The Schools 4−4−0s

'Steam Past' Books from Allen & Unwin

THE LIMITED by O. S. Nock
THE BIRTH OF BRITISH RAIL by Michael R. Bonavia
STEAM'S INDIAN SUMMER by George Heiron and Eric Treacy
GRAVEYARD OF STEAM by Brian Handley
PRESERVED STEAM IN BRITAIN by Patrick B. Whitehouse
MEN OF THE GREAT WESTERN by Peter Grafton
TRAVELLING BY TRAIN IN THE EDWARDIAN AGE by Philip Unwin
MAUNSELL'S NELSONS by D. W. Winkworth
MAN OF THE SOUTHERN: JIM EVANS LOOKS BACK by Jim Evans
TRAINS TO NOWHERE: BRITISH STEAM TRAIN ACCIDENTS 1906–1960 by J. A. B. Hamilton
TRAVELLING BY TRAIN IN THE 'TWENTIES AND 'THIRTIES by Philip Unwin
MEN OF THE LNER by Peter Grafton
A HISTORY OF THE LMS by O. S. Nock: I. The First Years, 1923–30
                                        II. The Record-Breaking 'Thirties, 1931–39
A HISTORY OF THE LNER by Michael R. Bonavia: I. The Early Years, 1923–33
                                        II. The Age of the Streamliners, 1934–39
ON AND OFF THE RAILS by Sir John Elliot
THE RIDDLES STANDARD TYPES AT WORK by G. Freeman Allen
THE SCHOOLS 4–4–0s by D. W. Winkworth
STEAM, a year book edited by Roger Crombleholme and Terry Kirtland

By the same author:
BULLEID'S PACIFICS

The Schools 4-4-0 s

D. W. Winkworth

London
GEORGE ALLEN & UNWIN
Boston   Sydney

George Allen & Unwin (Publishers) Ltd,
40 Museum Street, London WC1A 1LU, UK

George Allen & Unwin (Publishers) Ltd,
Park Lane, Hemel Hempstead, Herts HP2 4TE, UK

Allen & Unwin Inc.,
9 Winchester Terrace, Winchester, Mass 01890, USA

George Allen & Unwin Australia Pty Ltd,
8 Napier Street, North Sydney, NSW 2060, Australia

First published in 1982
Reprinted 1984

British Library Cataloguing in Publication Data

Winkworth, D. W.
    The Schools 4−4−0s.
1. Southern Railway Company − History
2. Locomotives − England − History
I. Title
625.2′61′0942   TJ603.4.G72.S67
ISBN 0−04−385095−2

Picture research by Mike Esau

Set in 10 on 12 point Bembo by Nene Phototypesetters Ltd
and printed in Great Britain
by Biddles Ltd, Guildford, Surrey

To the memory of
Gordon
recalling our days
spent admiring
Bournemouth's Schools

Contents

Illustrations

Tables

Preface

Ever since *Maunsell's Nelsons* appeared there has been a certain inevitability about this volume. The Lord Nelson design of locomotive in itself may have fallen short of its potential but, if nothing else, it did pave the way for the Schools class – Maunsell's jewel of a locomotive – and as such deserving of separate treatment in a book rather than sharing with other types as has mostly been the case hitherto. Thus the continuing development of Southern steam locomotive design is carried forward to another class and another volume.

With a success story to write about it is all too easy to eulogise, and the need to treat the subject objectively has always been in mind as well as to keep within the length allowed by the publisher. This second point will explain why detailed references to the final decade of the class could have been expanded; it was considered that, as this period is well documented in the railway press, preference should be given to less well-recorded events (such as the exhibition dates and wartime misfortunes) of the years when observers of the railway scene were fewer in number and restricted in scope. How successfully the first requirement has been met must remain for the reader to judge.

Acknowledgments

As customary with works of this nature it is wise to cast the net as widely as possible in gathering information and nowhere is this more necessary than in the performance realm. Unstinting help has been given by recorders and those holding such records; all those gentlemen whose names appear in the text as recorders of runs will have the satisfaction of their own particular contribution to this Schools class tribute. Additionally, the librarian of the Stephenson Locomotive Society kindly made available some of the late Norman Harvey's timings held in the library; Mr S. C. Nash provided the late R. A. H. Weight's notes on running between Polegate and Brighton; Mr K. J. Baker once more searched the notebooks of his deceased father for data; Mr R. N. Clements readily provided copious details from records made by his late brother and the editor of the *Railway Magazine* again permitted reference to runs which have appeared in past issues.

Besides researching official records at the Public Record Office and the National Railway Museum, York, general information has been provided by Lord Wolfenden, Messrs D. Cullum, J. R. Fairman, B. Fletcher, J. N. C. Law, S. C. Nash, G. O. P. Pearce, R. C. Riley, P. Trushell and E. S. Youldon (who also scrutinised parts of the text) and contact with staff or archivists at Christ's Hospital, Downside, Merchant Taylors, Uppingham, Wellington and Whitgift and some county libraries has proved helpful. Yet again Mr S. C. Nash read through the manuscript and made valuable suggestions. The author is happy to record his gratitude to all concerned for their help and encouragement.

I
Evolution

Some steam locomotive designs, such as Bulleid's Pacifics, were created; others, like Gresley's A4 class of streamliners, evolved. This is not, however, to equate boldness with inventiveness nor caution with slavery to tradition. As often as not circumstances dictate the course of action, which could well have been the situation so far as Maunsell's Schools class was concerned.

Appointed Chief Mechanical Engineer of the Southern Railway group upon its formation, R. E. L. Maunsell had made haste slowly in producing new designs, preferring rather to improve a good existing type before embarking upon an entirely new venture. Eventually, in the summer of 1926, the precursor of the Lord Nelson 4–6–0 class made its debut to be followed nearly two years later by further examples. This, Maunsell's largest ever essay (apart from stillborn projects) in express passenger locomotive design, was in response to the call by the traffic department for power to haul 500-ton trains at an average speed of 55 mph.

Another requirement by the traffic operators was for a type with an axle load of not more than 21 tons to deal with 400-ton trains at the same start-to-stop average speed of 55 mph. The L1 type of 4–4–0 (itself an extension of the earlier L class) constructed in 1926 – perhaps as a stop-gap measure – was capable of dealing with 350-ton trains at that rate on occasions, although that probably represented the absolute limit for the class. Something with greater power was called for, though not as large as the King Arthur 4–6–0 locomotives. The doubtful possibility of modifying the River 2–6–4 tank design by increasing the water-carrying capacity was dismissed when the track gave notice, in the shape of the Bearsted and Sevenoaks derailments, that it required overhaul and strengthening to be able to sustain the class as designed, let alone in a heavier guise.

So there was not much joy to be obtained in beefing-up existing designs. Carrying out the reverse exercise of scaling-down meant starting with the Lord Nelson drawings and this became the way the Southern Railway locomotive design staff tackled the problem. Omission of one inside cylinder, one pair of driving wheels and the shortening of the boiler was the logical process of reduction. Indeed that was the precise result of the exercise – a truncated Nelson in fact. The wheelbase worked out at 25 ft 6 in. and the markedly tapered boiler was 11 feet long with a firebox length of 8 ft 8 in.; grate area was 27 sq. ft, the heating surface totalled 1,863 sq. ft and with 220 lb/sq. in. boiler pressure a tractive effort figure of 25,130 lb. was arrived at, although an alternative pressure of 250 lb/sq. in. was given consideration.

All was not well, however, because the calculated axle weight came out at 22 tons which was

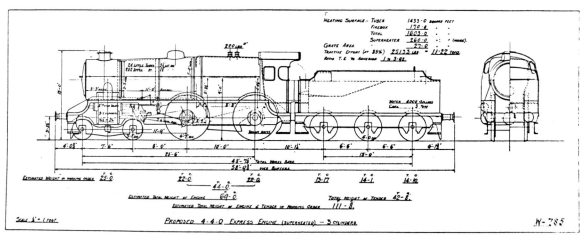

1. First thoughts on the design are recorded in this diagram which indicates a Belpaire-type firebox and an axle weight as high as 22 tons.

in excess of the maximum permitted by the civil engineer. Thus slimming-down was still necessary: nothing could be done in reducing further the number of axles and two-cylinder propulsion would have provided clearance troubles with large outside cylinders, so – as James Clayton (Maunsell's Personal Assistant) has stated – 'Mr Maunsell had to forego his predilection for the Belpaire firebox.'

With this obstacle removed a solution became apparent. The King Arthur type boiler with its round-topped firebox provided the answer and this was duly adapted for the new class. With the originally proposed Belpaire firebox design, an effort had been made to overcome the restricted clearances of the Tonbridge–Hastings via Battle route by raking the cab profile inwards, as well as the top of the tender sides, but the width of the firebox made forward vision from the cab so poor that it is extremely doubtful if this solution would have been acceptable. This problem did not arise with the round-topped firebox, and the distinctive cab became a distinguishing feature

of the engines which may have fostered the mistaken impression that the class was primarily built for the Hastings line.

With so many features taken from existing classes the design work did not present a lot of problems. Standard items such as boiler mountings, 6 ft 7 in. diameter driving wheels, the Lord Nelson class bogie, cylinders and sanding arrangements, had merely to be brought together and combined with newly designed frame, boiler and cab. The result was a pleasingly compact and robust looking locomotive which carried the unmistakable lineaments of the Southern Railway's motive power stable as exemplified by the King Arthur and Lord Nelson classes.

From these amendments to the original proposal, the design crystallised into an engine with a frame length of 32 ft 11 in. having a 10-foot rigid wheelbase, four driving wheels of 6 ft 7 in. diameter and three cylinders of 16½ inches diameter and 26 inches stroke driving the leading built-up single-throw crank axle. Three separate sets of Walschaerts valve gear were employed rather than a conjugated gear favoured at one stage. The diameter of the piston valves was

18

2.   The lineal descent of the Schools class from the Lord Nelson design is easy to recognise from these photographs of 'Sir Walter Raleigh' and 'Dulwich', and is accentuated by a common type of tender. Five of the first batch of Schools, including no. E907, were fitted with six-wheel tenders previously attached to King Arthur and Lord Nelson class engines.

3. In the shadow of Windsor Castle no. E900 'Eton' is inspected by members of Eton College in March 1930. In addition to a cast numberplate on the rear of the tender, the number also appeared on the buffer beam.

Lens of Sutton

8 inches with 1½-inch lap and ¼-inch lead, the same as for the Lord Nelsons. The leading bogie had 3 ft 1 in. diameter wheels and the minimum curve radius was 4.32 chains. Maximum overall width was 8 ft 6½ in. and the centre of gravity 5 ft 4 in.

The boiler barrel length was 11 ft 9 in. with a 9-foot long firebox, the length between the tube plates being 12 ft 2½ in.; overall boiler diameter was 5 ft 5¾ in. and the centre line 9 feet above rail level. There were 216 1¾-inch diameter and twenty-four 5¼-inch diameter tubes and a Maunsell-type superheater with relief valves. The firebox had a grate area – the grate being at a constant slope – of 28.3 sq. ft; heating surfaces were (all in square feet):

Firebox	162
Small tubes	1,205
Large tubes	399
Evaporative Total	1,766
Superheater	283
Total	2,049

Tractive effort (at 85 per cent boiler pressure of 220 lb/sq. in.) remained at the original design figure of 25,130 lb.

There was a cab window each side and other equipment included hand sanding, laminated springing, a three-feed sight lubricator, Gresham & Craven No. 11 live steam injector, Davies & Metcalfe No. 10 exhaust system type H injector, a 30-inch diameter vacuum cylinder mounted under the cab and a vacuum pump (5-in. x 26-in. stroke) actuated by the inside motion.

The weight of the locomotive was 67 tons 2 cwt with 21 tons on each driving axle, the factor of adhesion being 3.73. The tender was a standard six-wheel type of 4,000-gallon water and 5-ton coal capacity modified by having the side sheets turned inwards at the top for gauge profile purposes; sanding apparatus at the leading end was provided and the weight of 43 tons 8 cwt gave a combined weight for engine and tender in working order of 109½ tons. Without fuel and water the weights were 61 tons 19 cwt and 19 tons 11 cwt respectively to total 81½ tons.

20

It is not without interest to note that when the first of the class was weighed at Ashford works thirty years after its advent with 2 inches of water in the glass, 1,000 gallons of water and 3 tons of coal in the tender the weight was found to be 66 tons 19 cwt for the engine (with exactly 21 tons on each driving axle) and 30 tons 3 cwt for the tender, despite additions such as smoke deflectors, multiple-jet exhaust and large-diameter chimney and removal of the vacuum pump.

The combined length overall for engine and tender was 58 ft 9¾ in., and the design assumed the distinction of being the most powerful passenger 4-4-0 type not only in Britain but also in Europe.

At the Rolling Stock Committee meeting on 23 March 1928 it was recommended that twenty-five passenger tender engines be ordered. A breakdown into types – other than passenger tender – was not made but the result noted under the heading of 'Orders Outstanding' at the March 1929 meeting was five Lord Nelsons, ten V class 4-4-0s and ten U1 class 2-6-0s.

The last Lord Nelson order for five engines was carried out during September, October and November 1929 and then, after a short break, the first engine of order No. 378, no. E900 'Eton' emerged from Eastleigh works in March 1930 to be followed, at the rate of two a month, by the remaining nine engines which were to complete the first order for ten V or, as they were to be more commonly referred to, Schools class locomotives, each costed at £6,092.

Although the ten locomotives were uniform the tenders, rather curiously, were not: the five tenders attached to nos E900–E904 were new construction but the remaining five had seen use in straight-sided condition behind no. E852 'Sir Walter Raleigh' and King Arthurs nos E768, E770, E771 and E772 during the experiment of using 4,000-gallon tenders on some members of these classes on the Eastern Section. Whereas the standard Schools class tenders had one edge of the framing of the front and rear steps concave, these five tenders had both edges straight and this became a readily recognisable feature. Whether these tenders were stripped to the underframes and given a new superstructure or,

21

5.   The early members of the class were divided between Deal and Eastbourne sheds to work services to and from London. Here no. E904 'Lancing' approaches Clapham Junction with an Eastbourne-bound train complete with some Pullman cars.

as would appear more likely, were altered by turning in the side sheets at the top with modification to the intermediate bulkheads, is not entirely clear. In any event these five retained the old-style steps throughout their career and were numbered in with the general series of Schools tenders which began at 700, locomotive no. E900 taking tender 700, no. E901 tender 701 and so on. Boiler numbers, incidentally, ran from 807 to 816, again attached in strict order from no. E900 onwards.

Naming ceremonies, as such, were not indulged in. The opportunity was taken, however, to place each member of the class on view at the home station of the school concerned, when the scholars and members of the general public were able to make an inspection, and in at least one instance (Sherborne) it is recorded that the engine moved up and down the siding with the boys riding on the tender. These exhibitions took place as follows:

Locomotive	Exhibited At	Date (1930)
E900 'Eton'	Waterloo	26 March
	Windsor & Eton	28/29 March
E901 'Winchester'	Winchester	9/10 May
E902 'Wellington'	Crowthorne	30/31 May

6. No. E901 'Winchester' passes Chelsfield on a down Deal train complete with Pullman in the summer of 1931. By this time the engine had the two lamp irons on the smokebox moved onto the smokebox door, and sanding to the rear pair of coupled wheels had been introduced, as witness the sand-box beneath the running plate and between the driving wheels, the filler cap being just visible behind the splasher to the leading coupled wheel. The style of numerals used on the buffer beam was peculiar, so far as the Schools were concerned, to the first two members of the class.

E903 'Charterhouse'	Farncombe	13/14 June
E904 'Lancing'	Lancing	27/28 June
E905 'Tonbridge'	Tonbridge	4/5 July
E906 'Sherborne'	Sherborne	18/19 July
E907 'Dulwich'	Herne Hill	25/26 July
E908 'Westminster'	Waterloo	6 October
E909 'St. Paul's'	Waterloo	14/15 October

That these engines should appear without smoke deflectors seems odd, the more so as the five Lord Nelsons built a few months previously had been so fitted following the general application to that class in the spring of 1929 and the approval that had been given in June of that year for sixty-one engines of classes H15 and S15 to be treated likewise. Eventually smoke deflectors were fitted but meanwhile some members had the two lamp irons protruding from the smoke-box moved onto the smokebox door to avoid obstructing the forward view from the cab when route discs were carried.

Other amendments which were made included the fitting of sanding gear to the rear pair of driving wheels (the Schools had been treated in the same way as the Lord Nelsons with sanding to the leading driving wheels only), as well as changing from gravity to steam operation to overcome difficulties with track circuits by the over-generous discharge of sand; the dropping of the 'E' prefix to the numbers in mid-1931 which was, of course, a matter of policy and not peculiar to the class; and the alteration to the

23

bogie by the substitution of coil type springs for the leaf type, but which was not completed before no. 902 had suffered a fracture on 21 October 1933.

The first members of the class made their appearance working Bournemouth line services so that Eastleigh works could attend to any shortcomings that became manifest. Nothing of serious import happened and so, on 26 April 1930, nos E900 and E901 made their debut at Charing Cross on Folkestone and Dover line services, with others following in due course. As the Hastings (via Battle) route had not been upgraded to take the class, it was decided to split the ten members between Deal (a sub-shed of Dover) and Eastbourne locomotive depots. Nos E900 to E903, E905 and E906 went to Deal, the remainder to Eastbourne: the Deal engines took over the fast duties to Charing Cross via Tonbridge which had been the preserve of the L1 class 4–4–0s and the ill-fated River tanks, and had no difficulty in dealing with nine-coach 300-ton trains, especially over the Ashford–Tonbridge portion of the journey where high speed was often enjoyed. The Eastbourne-based engines did not have the same opportunity for spectacular running but nonetheless established themselves well on the Victoria road and – because they could be accommodated on the turntable at New Cross Gate shed – London Bridge services. Deal shed was closed in September 1930 and the six Schools were then transferred to the new Ramsgate shed.

By the end of June 1931 the modification of curves and reballasting of the track between Tunbridge Wells Central and Hastings had progressed far enough to allow the class regularly to use the route. Accordingly the Schools were introduced as from 5 July 1931 to the services with which they were always to be primarily associated and over which they were destined to hold sway for over a quarter of a century. On 6 July no. E904 headed the 10.25 am ex Charing Cross which had two Pullman cars occupied by a party of Southern Railway officers, including the chairman, general manager, directors and heads of departments (such as Mr Maunsell), travelling down for the official opening of the new station at Hastings. The 390-ton train left London ten minutes late of which five were recouped by the time Hastings was reached, despite the heavy load for the route and the permanent way restrictions still in force. The 4.55 pm return train carrying the party was handled by no. E909.

Eastbourne shed had to relinquish the four engines it had had for about a year for work on the Hastings services, and to take new U1 class 2–6–0s in their stead. Clearly more engines of the Schools class were desirable because four engines at St Leonards shed did not constitute a large enough strength for speedier timings to be drawn up, especially as the six locomotives allocated to Ramsgate were needed for the fast Folkestone trains. The engines had made their mark and were obviously set for a steady career; all this had been anticipated by the Rolling Stock Committee which had authorised, at its meeting on 19 March 1931, the construction of a further twenty members of the class.

2
Expansion

Financial stringency in the early 1930s decreed that investment, no less on the railways than elsewhere, should be made only in cases which provided a certain and immediate return and, accordingly, no great haste was evident in proceeding with the second order of Schools engines. This did not reflect any shortcomings in the design; on the contrary, indicator trials made with no. E909 between London Bridge and Eastbourne in the first quarter of 1931 gave satisfactory results. With a loading of 345 tons, coal (Chislet 14500BTU) consumption was 51 lb. per train mile, the highest IHP figure of 1176 was recorded at 46 mph, and the absolute maximum figure calculated as being just short of 1300 IHP.

Meanwhile, the locomotive renumbering scheme started in mid-1931 meant that the 'E' prefix to the locomotive numbers (denoting Eastleigh as the works responsible for repairs) would be dropped at the first opportunity. Later in the year the fitting of smoke deflectors to the class began, the addition of which made for a rather more puissant appearance and was thought by some to be a distinct improvement to the lines of the engines.

July 1931 had seen the whole class concentrated on the Eastern Section and, because of this, the occasional difficulties encountered in restarting heavy trains in the up direction on the awkward rising curve of the then platform 7 at London Bridge became more numerous. To overcome this several experiments were conducted on the lead of the piston valves, the engines involved being nos 906 and 907; the result of these 1932 experiments was to standardise on a 1/4-inch lead, measured from the edge of the ring instead of at the valve head.

Construction of order 631 for the twenty additional members had been proceeding at Eastleigh during 1932 when suddenly, in December, nos 910 to 914 were released to traffic. The cost was recorded as £5,374 each. The engines were standard with the others of the class with one exception, namely the position of the cab windows and size of look-out cut-outs. The latter were increased in height from 2 ft 1 3/4 in. to 2 ft 8 in. and the cab windows, still the same size, were moved upwards 6 1/4 inches so that the top edge of the window lined up with the top edge of the look-out. The tenders varied only from the first batch of five by having rolled steel disc wheels instead of the spoked variety and a bank of tool and crew lockers right across the front end.

Names were allocated thus:

910	'Merchant Taylors'
911	'Dover'
912	'Downside'
913	'Christ's Hospital'
914	'Eastbourne'

Three of these engines were placed on display

J. Scrace Collection

7. Indicator trials were conducted on the Waterloo–Salisbury route and between London and Eastbourne early in 1931. No. E909 was the engine concerned, and is seen here with the shelter erected around the smokebox for the purpose.

to the public and, more particularly, to the boys of the schools concerned. For this purpose no. 911 appeared at Dover Priory on 28 February and 1 March 1933 while nos 913 and 914 were exhibited at their home stations on 15 March and 28 March 1933, respectively. Expectations of Downside Abbey School seeing no. 912 locally were, however, unfulfilled as the April 1933 number of *The Raven* (the school magazine) makes clear: 'Unfortunately owing to its size it was unable to come to Chilcompton to be inspected by the school, as had been arranged, but it will take the school train up to London at the end of term.' No record has been found to confirm that no. 912 did work the special train

(presumably from Templecombe) but that is not to say that the promise was not honoured; the likely date was 17 April 1933 deriving from the Downside tradition of the term ending on Easter Monday so that Holy Week could be celebrated together.

These first five engines of the second order were allocated to Eastbourne – with the exception of no. 912 which went to Ramsgate to join the members of the class removed from Deal – for work on the London services. A more gradual release to traffic of the next five of the class was made, the names and dates being:

915	'Brighton'	May 1933
916	'Whitgift'	June 1933
917	'Ardingly'	June 1933
918	'Hurstpierpoint'	July 1933
919	'Harrow'	July 1933

Nos 915 and 916 had a minor, though distinctive, alteration to their chimneys, which were without capuchins (the front lip). Harrow, not being on the Southern Railway, did not have the customary opportunity to inspect its 'own' locomotive; the other four engines did participate in such events, no. 915 at Brighton on 10 and 11 October, no. 916 at West Croydon on 18 July, no. 917 at Ardingly on 17 October and no. 918 at Hassocks on 24 October, all in the year of their construction.

The first two members of this quintet were dispatched to Eastbourne to enable nos 910 and 911 to be sent over to Ramsgate, which in turn released nos 903, 905 and 906 to St Leonards so that for the summer of 1933 the disposition of the class was:

Eastbourne shed: 913 to 916
St Leonards shed: 903 to 909, 917 and 918
Ramsgate shed: 900 to 902, 910 to 912 and 919

The remaining ten of this order were released in like manner to the first ten – five at the end of the year and the others in the summer following – thus:

During 1933
920	'Rugby'	November
921	'Shrewsbury'	November
922	'Marlborough'	December
923	'Uppingham'	December
924	'Haileybury'	December

During 1934
925	'Cheltenham'	May
926	'Repton'	June
927	'Clifton'	June
928	'Stowe'	June
929	'Malvern'	August

As all these engines took the names of schools remote from the Southern Railway system there

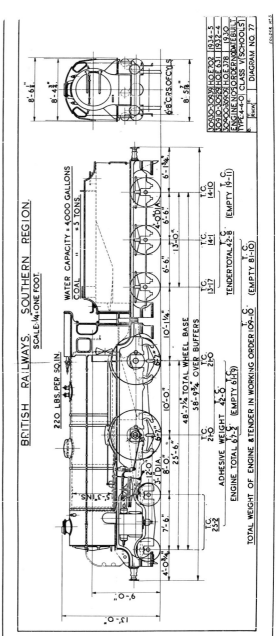

8. Diagram of the class as built.

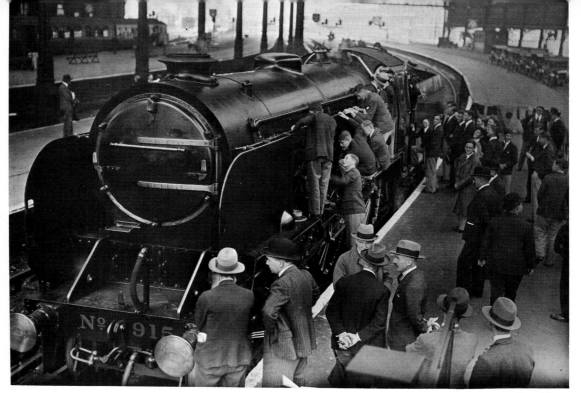

9. No. 915 'Brighton' being inspected at Brighton on 10 October 1933. This engine, together with no. 916, was turned out from Eastleigh works at the time of construction with a chimney not having a capuchin. Other engines which carried similar chimneys during part of their existence included nos 901, 904 and 924.

were no exhibitions. However, this did not prevent no. 923 becoming involved in a curious incident with regard to its name.

Uppingham's Headmaster Owen took strong exception to a railway locomotive carrying the school's name, despite Major Eric Gore-Browne (an SR director) being a trustee of the school; he had probably thought that everyone concerned would be pleased. Owen was opposed, almost to a point of fanaticism, to any form of self-advertisement and this must have been a particular affront to him after his passionate denunciations on the subject to his pupils – hence his protest. His demand for removal of the offending nameplates was met,

indeed replaced by those commemorating Bradfield but, ironically, the change did not take place until August 1934 by which time Headmaster Wolfenden (later Lord Wolfenden) was at the helm. Oddly, in view of this furore, the school has one of the original nameplates in its possession!

Of this batch of ten engines, nos 920 and 921 went to Ramsgate, nos 922 and 923 to St Leonards, the remainder being allocated to Fratton shed for Waterloo–Portsmouth services which was new ground for the class.

Order 702, which the Rolling Stock Committee had sanctioned at its meeting on 1 March 1932, comprising ten locomotives, was then started on by Eastleigh works. These engines were produced at a cost of £5,256 each for nos 930 to 934 and £5,209 each for the last five, the numbers, names and dates to traffic being:

28

D. W. Winkworth Collection

10. This view of the no. 921 'Shrewsbury' indicates how the backs of the tenders were treated for nos 910 to 939, and may be compared with illustration 3. The ten engines of the first order were brought into line after the 'E' prefix to the numbers was dropped in mid-1931.

930	'Radley'	December 1934
931	'King's-Wimbledon'	January 1935
932	'Blundell's'	February 1935
933	'King's-Canterbury'	March 1935
934	'St. Lawrence'	March 1935
935	'Sevenoaks'	June 1935
936	'Cranleigh'	June 1935
937	'Epsom'	July 1935
938	'St Olave's'	July 1935
939	'Leatherhead'	August 1935

The name of no. 939 was proposed as 'St Johns Leatherhead' but presumably it was discovered that a two-line nameplate would be necessary and so a shortened version was preferred.

With several of the schools comprising this batch coming within Southern Railway territory, the custom of exhibiting the engines was revived. The first of these viewings took place at Wimbledon on 15 February 1935 when no. 931 was displayed, followed on 19 June by no. 933 at Canterbury West, no. 934 at Ramsgate (24 June), no. 935 at Sevenoaks Tubs Hill (1 July), and no. 938 at London Bridge (22 July); on 1 & 2 October a couple of two-day events involving nos 937 and 939 were held at Epsom and Leatherhead respectively and, finally, no. 936 – having been given special dispensation to travel over the branch normally prohibited to

11. No. 923 'Uppingham' calling at Wadhurst with a down Hastings train in 1934 before Headmaster Owen had succeeded in having his school's name removed. The engine was rechristened 'Bradfield' in August of that year.

the class – visited Cranleigh for display on 26 October.

Nos 930 to 933 were sent to Fratton to complete that shed's allocation of the class, the other six engines going to Bricklayers Arms shed. During the time that some of these engines were being placed in service there came an emergency when a barge hit Southerham bridge (just east of Lewes) on 5 April 1935, causing enough damage to the structure for a severe speed restriction to be placed immediately on trains crossing the bridge as well as a total prohibition on the King

Arthur class. To fill the gap left by the withdrawal of the largest passenger engines on the Eastbourne services a few Schools were requisitioned from St Leonards and Ramsgate and sent to Stewarts Lane shed. These included nos 902, 910, 915, 919 and 930. The class remained on these duties until full electric services to Eastbourne were inaugurated on 7 July 1935.

Main line electrification was now the priority of the Southern Railway's traction policy and so when no. 939 emerged from Eastleigh works in August 1935 it proved to be the last of the class to be built. The forty engines then entered a stable period of two years divided between four sheds: St Leonards had the first dozen of the class, Ramsgate shed the next twelve, Fratton

National Railway Museum

John F. W. Paige

12. There were three Schools engines which carried the contraction St for Saint in their names. The nameplates of nos 909 and 934 had a half-height 'T' followed by a stop whereas those of no. 938 (lower) were unique for the class in having a half-height 'T' set high without a stop as had been the case with no. 856 'Lord St Vincent' of the Lord Nelson class.

the following ten with the remainder at Bricklayers Arms, covering duties that would otherwise require St Leonards or Ramsgate based locomotives to be stabled overnight in the London area. The year closed with a further amendment of the piston valve lead having been made – this time to ³⁄₁₆ inch.

Acceleration tests carried out on the Hastings route early in 1936 brought no alteration to the timetables nor did experiments with two different types of axle boxes for the tenders of the class have any lasting effect. No. 908 'Westminster' had Isothermos type axle boxes fitted to tender 708 in June 1932 and these obviously proved satisfactory and gave good service until replacement by the standard type in April 1951. The SKF type axle boxes fitted to tenders 714 and 726 did not fare anything like so well. Tender 726 appeared new with the SKF type coupled to locomotive no. 926 in June 1934 and tender 714, attached to no. 914 'Eastbourne', was altered about March 1935 but neither lasted in that condition for very long, reversion to the standard type being in February and June 1936, respectively. Both Isothermos and SKF versions of axle box appeared circular when viewed broadside compared with the smaller standard oblong fitting.

No. 914 suffered a further experiment when it acquired, in February 1937, a Sinuflo superheater. This followed the incorporation of that type of superheater in the large boiler fitted to Lord Nelson class no. 857 a month previously. Again nothing came out of the alteration. Arising out of a decision which affected all classes on the railway, the vacuum pumps, actuated by the inside cylinder crosshead, were removed from the Schools.

In May 1936 two more spare boilers (1040 and 1041) had been commissioned, making a total of forty-four for the class of forty engines. Initially boilers 807 to 816 were attached, in order, to engines nos 900 to 909, boilers 1011 to 1030 to nos 910 to 929, boilers 1009 and 1010 to nos 930 and 931, 1031 to 1033 to nos 932 to 934 and 1035 to 1039 were paired with nos 935 to 939. Spare boilers 1007 and 1034 were produced in March 1932 and March 1935, respectively. With the 10 per cent excess, the float of boilers available obviated an engine in works waiting for its own boiler to be repaired (a process which took

National Railway Museum

13. A short-lived experiment in the thirties was the fitting of two tenders with SKF axle boxes. No. 914 'Eastbourne' illustrated here was one engine with such a tender, no. 926 'Repton' being the other.

longer than overhaul of the rest of the locomotive) and so got back into traffic quicker. In consequence a boiler, unlike a tender, would not stay wedded to one locomotive.

With the main line electrification to Portsmouth Harbour due to operate from July 1937 it was obvious that the ten representatives of the Schools at Fratton shed would have to be employed elsewhere. Consequently no. 929 from that depot found itself, in the out-of-season period at the end of 1936, on loan to Bournemouth shed and working a variety of turns to Waterloo (including the winter-formation 'Bournemouth Belle' on one occasion) as well as through trains to Oxford. What was more surprising, in view of the 4,000-gallon water

capacity of the tender and the limits that imposed on non-stop running, was the approbation of the Bournemouth drivers for the class. So the way was paved for the transfer of the whole of the Fratton contingent (nos 924 to 933) to Bournemouth in July 1937 to displace the King Arthurs and with it the peculiar reversion in the haulage of a main line's express trains from 4–6–0 to 4–4–0 power.

The whole exercise was a complete success apart from the services to and from Oxford for which the Great Western Railway, being unused to such large four-coupled engines, vetoed their employment. For these through trains a couple of King Arthurs had to return. Mr Maunsell remained in office just long enough to see his finest design performing regularly and with distinction on the Bournemouth route before handing over in September 1937 to his successor from another company, Mr O. V. Bulleid.

3
Bulleid Era

Because of more pressing demands elsewhere the Schools did not receive immediate scrutiny upon Mr Bulleid's accession to the Chief Mechanical Engineer's chair of the Southern Railway. Apart from some tests on live and exhaust steam pressure in the cylinders conducted on the Hastings route in June 1938 with no. 901, which was fitted with an indicator shelter for the purpose, the changes in his first year were mainly what would today be termed cosmetic.

A brighter livery had been propounded for the Southern Railway's locomotives and carriages before Bulleid had arrived and an experiment had been carried out on at least one electric multiple main line set on the Central Section employing a light yellowish-green. Bulleid turned out his first new design on the Southern, the buffet cars for the Bognor electrified service, in a rather more pleasing shade of green with less yellow in it which later came to rejoice in the term malachite.

There seems, however, to have been a desire to 'keep up with the Jones's' of the other railway companies. In the mid and late 'thirties streamlining was very much the vogue, extending beyond cars and railway trains to static objects, such as buildings and furniture, and, as Bulleid had been very much involved with the introduction of streamlined locomotives and trains on the LNER, it was natural that his thoughts would turn to this as a medium to project the

Southern's image to the public. It was not much use trying out any ideas on the Lord Nelsons because of their inconsistent performance which was under investigation at the time, so the only alternative was to experiment with a Schools. This Bulleid did.

No. 935 'Sevenoaks', which had been taken into Eastleigh works on 22 March 1938 for overhaul, acted as a guinea-pig. Following proposals drawn up the previous month two distinct – but not dissimilar – designs were tried using a combination of materials such as plywood and canvas on suitable framing. As will be observed from illustration 15, the principal differences were that the second proposal had smoke deflectors and an irregular-shaped casing forward of the leading pair of driving wheels (instead of a continuous skirt), and a more striking lining-out arrangement for the livery, as well as a different position for the 'SOUTHERN' plate. The engine's name failed to appear anywhere. Common to both designs were the numberplate on the cab side, the number 999 and the removal of the cylinder drain pipes, and the leading steps on the engine. The remaining steps still retained the standard lining-out. There was no provision for lamp irons and this, coupled with the absence of a cab look-out (the windows were dummies), was indicative of a mock-up rather than a working experiment.

One wonders how the driver liked the trial run which is reported to have taken place from

14. Early in the regime of Mr Bulleid, cylinder steam pressure observations were made with no. 901 'Winchester' – seen here at Cannon Street in July 1938 on the 6.15 pm to Ramsgate via Chatham during the period of examination. The chimney without a lip will be noted, and also a painting variation in the lining-out of the cylinder casing in a panel.

Eastleigh to Micheldever and back. It might be argued that this was not so much an attempt to streamline a Schools (the unbending civil engineer would never have sanctioned the extra weight) as an exercise in outlines for Bulleid's new design. Certainly some of the sketches for the proposed 2–8–2 and, later, 4–6–2 bore a remarkable affinity to no. 999.

No. 935 was released from Eastleigh works on 13 April 1938 in its original state and then, two months later, came the result of the livery deliberations. Within the space of ten days, six of Bournemouth shed's Schools came back from Eastleigh resplendent in the new Bournemouth green with new style lettering and numerals. This green later became known as malachite but was first given the name of the route on which it made its debut as was the case with the olive- (or Dover) green. No. 929 arrived first on 29 June quickly followed by nos 930, 925, 927, 928 and 932 in that order; of these nos 929 and 932 were in works for repairs but

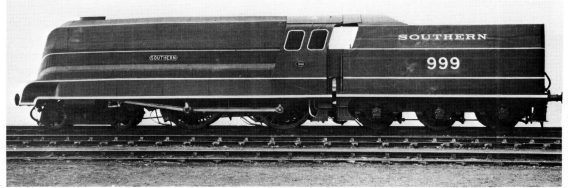

15. Streamlining mock-ups applied to no. 935 which was dubbed no. 999 for the occasion. These had no influence on the Schools class although providing a pointer to what Mr Bulleid's new engine might be expected to look like.

the others were specially called in for repainting. At the same time the carriage works was busy refurbishing coaching stock with seating having individual backs, and generally improving the interiors as well as repainting externally to match the engine livery, so that in early July there was a noticeable brightening-up of the trains forming many of the Waterloo–Bournemouth–Weymouth services. These included the 'Bournemouth Limited' (7.45 am ex Weymouth and 4.30 pm return from Waterloo), which necessitated the Bournemouth engine working a night goods train to Weymouth to enable it to take the up train, duty 381 (7.25 am

D. W. Winkworth

16. In June/July 1938 no. 932 was one of six engines turned out in the new Bournemouth green livery which later was known as malachite-green. Additionally it had its tender modified with high-sided sheets, and the company name was set higher than the numerals on the side of the cab instead of in line as was the case with the other Schools class engines with the new lettering. 'Blundell's' is depicted at Bournemouth Central with an up train.

Bournemouth West to Waterloo, 12.30 pm return to Weymouth and 6.30 pm Weymouth–Bournemouth Central) as well as duty 388, a turn which comprised the 1.1 pm Bournemouth Central–Weymouth, 5.37 pm up to Waterloo and the following day's 8.30 am Waterloo–Bournemouth Central.

To ensure a good turn-out, an additional gang of carriage cleaners took up work at Weymouth. The Bournemouth engines were kept in pristine condition with burnished buffers and some even had a burnished central star on the smokebox door. Assisted by the provision of better coal no less than the pride engendered by operating

these revamped trains, the Bournemouth foot-platemen, to their credit, rose to the occasion and gave excellent performances.

No. 932 had returned to Bournemouth in July not only in the new livery but with its tender (732) converted to self-trimming complete with higher side sheets, along similar lines to the Lord Nelson tenders that had been and were being modified at the time. Doubtless because the problem of the coal not working forward on the Lord Nelsons (which had prompted the self-trimming tenders) was not present on the Schools the alteration was not extended to the other thirty-nine tenders.

The next matter to receive attention was the fitting of speed recorders. It was intended that thirty of the Schools should have the Flaman type incorporating a moving roll which recorded the speed during the journey and which could be removed at the shed for examination as

36

17.   The first Schools to be fitted with the Lemaitre type multiple-jet exhaust and large-diameter chimney was no. 914 in January 1939. In view of the experimental nature of the fitment a stovepipe chimney was used initially.

required, as well as giving a visual indication while the locomotive was in motion. In the event rather less than thirty of the class were equipped, principally because of the outbreak of hostilities; fitting of these recorders began in October 1938 but not before a speed indicator (or speedometer), rather than a recorder, of the Stone-Deuta type had been attached to no. 939 in the previous August. Operation of this speedometer was by means of a flexible cable through a non-reversible gearbox fitted to a return crank on the left-hand rear coupled wheel (in much the same way as the type adopted by British Railways years later), with the indicator electrically operated and placed above the reversing-screw in the cab. Unfortunately, the accuracy of this instrument left something to be desired and in due course, after allegedly giving false readings in excess of 100 mph, it was discarded.

Little else of remark occurred during 1938 except for the establishment of the class on Royal Train specials, such as no. 915 on 19 and 22 July, when the King and Queen made a State visit to Paris using Victoria Station in London en route to and from Dover Marine, and no. 939 officiating on 15 November when King Carol of Rumania, accompanied by Crown Prince Michael, travelled over the same route to London. The special train conveying the President of France and Mme Lebrun from Dover Marine to Victoria on 21 March 1939 and the return on 24 March was another suitable duty

37

18. No. 934, fitted with the nameplates 'Westminster', between Bromley South and Bickley on the 9.55 am Victoria–Dover Marine French Presidential special train on 24 March 1939, with miniature flags fluttering on top of the headcode discs.

19. The first Schools locomotive to have the large-diameter chimney which was to become standard for the class was no. 931 'King's-Wimbledon'. This was the only engine in the original style livery to carry such a fitment. As far back as April 1932 a drawing had been made for fitting the class with Smith's speed recorders but in the event it was the Flaman type which was adopted. Part of this apparatus is clearly seen by the rear coupled wheel, which was to be fitted to just over twenty of the engines.

20. No. 937 'Epsom', seen at Nine Elms on 11 June 1939, was fitted with modified cylinders, modified multiple-jet exhaust and large-diameter chimney, and extended smokebox, as well as being altered for balancing. Eventually it reverted to the standard cylinders and standard modified exhaust, but not before putting up some excellent performances in traffic.

for the class, and accordingly no. 934 'St. Lawrence' recently out of works in new style lettering, albeit in the sage-green livery, was selected to work the train. Particular attention was given to the turn-out of the engine, even to the point that the white route indicator discs were each surmounted with a pair of miniature Union flags. The name 'St. Lawrence' had no particular significance so far as the railway authorities were concerned until someone with a feeling for history pointed out that one of France's finest overseas possessions – Quebec – was lost to the British above the waters of the

St Lawrence river. A hasty exchange of name-plates was effected with no. 908 'Westminster' which was not entirely inappropriate as M. Lebrun received an Address from the City of Westminster on the day of his arrival and had several engagements within its boundaries. One wonders, none the less, if any Frenchman even noticed the name. The period of exchange of nameplates was 19 to 25 March.

As may be gathered, the malachite-green livery was not having universal application to the class. After the advent of the malachite-green on the Bournemouth engines, the old sage-green combined with new type letters and figures became the standard for a period followed by an isolated case of the experimental olive-green, before there was a move over to malachite-green involving varying lining-out schemes as described in detail in chapter 9.

Meanwhile Bulleid had been very active on the Lord Nelsons, and by early 1939, after much empirical work, he had obtained a satisfactory multiple-jet exhaust arrangement coupled with a large-diameter chimney, and as this fitment had considerably improved performance with the class it was decided to extend its use to the Schools. As it was not unlikely that there might be an initial difficulty arising with the application of the new exhaust, the first member to be treated – no. 914 in late January 1939 – had the ugly stovepipe chimney fitted, the ugliness being accentuated by the greater height in comparison with that used on the Nelsons. The standard five-jet Lemaitre exhaust fitting, however, proved satisfactory without great modification and reports of enhanced performance soon flowed in. This allowed general modification of the class to start in July with no. 931 which was the first to have a chimney with lipped top and become the sole member to have a large-diameter chimney while retaining the old style livery and lettering.

There was another appearance of a stovepipe chimney on a Schools, nevertheless. This was on no. 937 'Epsom' in conjunction with cylinder experiments. Bulleid had been engaged on improving the steam passages of the cylinders of the Lord Nelson class and in May 1939 he fitted no. 937 with modified cylinders which necessitated setting forward the multiple-jet exhaust at an angle of about six degrees from the vertical and adapting the chimney by also setting it at an angle and then cutting off the top to give a line parallel to the boiler. This brought the chimney very close to the front of the smokebox, and to overcome this difficulty a 15-inch extension to the smokebox was made. About the same time alteration was made to the balancing weights in the driving wheels to give balance for revolving masses only, introducing in the process crude-looking weights when compared with the neat originals. Trials took place on the Western and Eastern Sections with excellent results, as is demonstrated in the next chapter.

Yet another alteration, made generally to the class, was effected to the piston valve lead which now became $1/8$-inch. So with his problem of the Lord Nelsons solved and those remedies extended to the Schools – although with far less need and only marginal benefit because of a satisfactory basic design – Bulleid was free to turn to new creations. Indeed the good result of the balancing experiment on no. 937 led to reciprocating balance being omitted from his Pacific engine.

In the event, modified cylinders were never introduced to the Schools and no more than half the class obtained the Lemaitre exhaust fitment – such were just two of the consequences of the declaration of war in September 1939.

4
Pre-War Performance

Chronologically, as well as geographically, a survey of pre-war performance is best served by working from east to west. Opening the running, therefore, is the Folkestone route which was the first to see the class at work. The seventy-mile run had its most taxing stretch in the 11½-mile climb out of the London basin from New Cross to Knockholt, after which came a downhill plunge to the crossing of the river Medway at Tonbridge, where there was a substantial speed restriction, followed by the long, straight run to Ashford and Folkestone. The schedule for the non-stop trains was 80 minutes although in table 1 no. 900 fittingly comes first (in detail A) with the 1.15 pm train from Charing Cross, first stop Ashford, which was allowed 66 minutes for the 56.1 miles. The early part of the run was hindered by a permanent way restriction but this did not affect the climb through Elmstead Woods, made at 37 mph; at Orpington the speed had increased to 51 mph, falling back to 42 mph at Knockholt summit, all these figures being typical for the class on the route. Downhill 70 mph was attained at Dunton Green and the maximum for the journey – 76 mph – was registered at Hildenborough. The time lost by the check before New Cross had been regained by Tonbridge and another minute was gained by Ashford after a maximum of 67 mph on that length.

In detail B of this table no. 902 gave a rather more fluctuating display. Because there was a temporary speed restriction to be observed just before Tonbridge it was understandable that an effort would be made to better the schedule before the slack was encountered. By Chislehurst nearly two minutes had been gained only to be halved on the rest of the climb to Knockholt. By Paddock Wood, however, the train was again just ahead of schedule and, with steadier running, arrival at Folkestone Central was 1¼ minutes early. The next run, in detail C, moves onto the middle of the period under review and features no. 916, one of the second batch of engines, on the Saturdays-only 12.55 pm from Charing Cross. Again consistent running, much as was to be expected on this route, was observed with 38 mph at Elmstead Woods, 49 mph at Orpington, 45 mph at Knockholt, 72 mph at Dunton Green, 78 mph at Hildenborough and a maximum of 71 mph east of Tonbridge.

The last of the four runs in table 1 was timed by Mr H. T. Clements on 3 July 1939, the train being the 7.15 pm from Charing Cross which had a timing of 80 minutes *inclusive* of a stop at Waterloo. No. 922 got a bad road at the junctions leading to London Bridge taking as long to pass that station from Waterloo as no. 902 had taken from Charing Cross in detail B. Admittedly no. 922's load was slightly less than the others under consideration but the 12-minute climb from Hither Green to Knockholt was fine with 52 mph being noted at Orpington. Maximum speeds were 76 mph at Hildenborough and 73 mph at Staplehurst and the 40½ miles from Tonbridge to Folkestone took no more than 39 minutes. For this excellent run net time for the 69.2 miles from Waterloo was 74 minutes.

Table 1. CHARING CROSS – FOLKESTONE CENTRAL

Detail		A	B	C	D
Locomotive no.		900	902	916	922
Vehicles		10	9	9	8
Tare load (tons)		299	278	282	254
Gross load (tons)		325	305	300	275

Mls		Sch.	m. s.	m. s.	m. s.	m. s.
0.0	CHARING CROSS	0	0 00	0 00	0 00	—
0.8	WATERLOO		—	—	2 25	0 00
						sigs
1.9	LONDON BRIDGE	5½	4 40	4 05	4 45	4 05
			pws		sigs	
4.9	New Cross	9½	10 05	8 15	10 09	8 05
7.2	Hither Green	12½	12 55	10 40	13 02	11 00
9.0	Grove Park		15 20	12 55	15 28	—
11.2	Chislehurst	18	18 45	16 10	18 54	16 25
13.8	ORPINGTON	21	22 10	19 50	22 14	19 40
16.6	Knockholt		25 40	24 00	25 48	23 00
20.6	Dunton Green		29 50	28 40	29 56	27 30
						pws
22.1	SEVENOAKS T.H.	31	31 10	30 10	31 18	29 45
27.0	Hildenborough		35 40	35 00	35 41	34 40
				pws		
29.5	TONBRIDGE★	38½	38 20	39 00	38 02	37 25
34.8	Paddock Wood	44½	44 30	44 10	43 15	43 15
39.4	Marden		48 40	48 00	47 14	47 00
41.9	Staplehurst	51	51 00	50 10	49 28	49 10
45.3	Headcorn		53 55	53 05	52 26	52 00
50.5	Pluckley		59 00	58 15	57 17	56 45
56.1	ASHFORD	65	65 00	63 55	62 33	61 40
60.4	Smeeth			68 35	66 48	65 45
					pws	
65.4	Sandling Junc.	75		74 15	75 10	70 50
69.3	Shorncliffe			—	79 02	74 30
70.0	FOLKESTONE C.	80		78 50	80 08	76 25
Estimated net time (mins)			63	77½	76½	74

★Speed restriction

Up running on this route was usually pretty sporting. A fast run to Tonbridge was necessary before the permanent speed restriction at the London end of the station and then would come a spirited climb of the North Downs to Knockholt followed by an equally spirited dash through the outer suburban area until probably signals would check progress. No. 906 opens the running in detail A of table 2 with an eight-coach train of the 5.10 pm departure. With a maximum of 77 mph at Headcorn even time was achieved by Staplehurst to give a gain of two minutes by Tonbridge. This gain was held all the way up to Knockholt, the minimum

Table 2. FOLKESTONE CENTRAL – CHARING CROSS

Detail		A	B		C	D
Locomotive no.		906	903		922	917
Vehicles		8	10		9	11
Tare load (tons)		257	329		290	356
Gross load (tons)		275	355		305	390

Mls		Sch.	m. s.	m. s.	Sch.	m. s.	m. s.
0.0	FOLKESTONE C.	0	0 00	0 00	0	0 00	0 00
4.5	Sandling Junc.	8	7 45	8 15	7½	7 22	8 23
9.6	Smeeth		12 35	13 15		11 56	13 32
13.8	ASHFORD	17	16 10	16 40	16½	15 13	17 00
				pws			
19.5	Pluckley		21 10	23 40		19 39	21 47
24.7	Headcorn		25 20	28 35		23 37	25 59
28.1	Staplehurst		28 00	31 25		26 14	28 38
30.6	Marden		30 05	33 35		28 11	30 45
35.1	Paddock Wood	36	33 50	37 20	34½	31 48	34 30
40.4	TONBRIDGE★	41	38 55	42 10	39½	36 54	39 09
42.9	Hildenborough		43 05	46 35		40 38	43 18
47.8	SEVENOAKS T.H.	53	50 55	54 45	51½	47 45	50 29
49.4	Dunton Green		52 30	56 25		49 21	52 09
53.4	Knockholt	59	56 55	60 50		53 50	56 51
56.1	ORPINGTON	62	59 20	63 15	60	56 00	59 34
58.7	Chislehurst	64½	61 35	65 20	62½	58 12	61 39
60.9	Grove Park		63 30	67 05		60 14	63 31
62.8	Hither Green	68	65 10	68 40	66	61 23	65 06
65.1	New Cross	71	67 55	71 45	69	64 14	68 15
			sigs			sig. stop (2)	
68.1	LONDON BRIDGE★	75	74 00	76 00	73	72 17	72 36
						sig. stop	
69.2	WATERLOO		—	sigs	76	79 34	74 49
70.0	CHARING CROSS	80	78 30	82 45			
Estimated net time (mins)			76½	77½		72	74¾

★Speed restriction

43

21. No. E902 'Wellington' heads a Deal express near
Chelsfield in the first year or two of its life.

being 36 mph with 47 mph at Knockholt itself. With a maximum of 74 mph coming into London another minute was gained and, despite a signal check, there was an early arrival at Charing Cross.

With ten coaches no. 903 (detail B) made a slower start and suffered a permanent way relaying check at Pluckley, passing Tonbridge 1¼ minutes down; nothing could be gained on the climb but an on-time arrival might just have been made but for the dead stand outside Charing Cross. A speed of 34 mph was the minimum on the climb to Knockholt, which was passed at 48 mph, and the maximum beyond was 78 mph.

The other two runs in this table were made on the 80-minute schedule inclusive of a call at Waterloo. In detail C no. 922 was timed by Mr G. G. Elliot on the 11.10 am departure from Folkestone Central on a day of continuous drizzle. Right from the start driver Pemble drove with great verve; 81 mph after Smeeth got

the train through Ashford over a minute early and with a maximum of 80 mph at Headcorn the gain by Tonbridge was 2½ minutes. On the climb to Sevenoaks the minimum speed was 39 mph but by Orpington the train was back to even-time with the 56.1 miles run in 56 minutes and this was maintained as far as New Cross after which a series of signal checks and stops intervened. Finally there comes no. 917 loaded up to all but 400 tons. By Headcorn the speed reached 79 mph, even-time was attained just after Marden and the climb up through Hildenborough was taken at 43 mph falling to a minimum of 34 mph; the summit at Knockholt was breasted at 44 mph and with 75 mph at Grove Park the day was won, no. 917 stopping in Waterloo with 1¼ minutes in hand at an average speed of just over 55 mph start-to-stop. This clearly demonstrated that over a far-from-easy course the performance requirement of the operating department laid down at the time of design – 400 tons at 55 mph – was being attained in traffic.

The other main line entirely in Kent –

Table 3. MARGATE – VICTORIA

Detail	A	B	C
Date	2 May 1938	29 July 1937	1 July 1939
Locomotive no.	921	916	914 (L)
Vehicles	7	9	10
Tare load (tons)	232	296	323
Gross load (tons)	245	315	350
Driver	Ovenden (RAM)	Ovenden (RAM)	Ovenden (RAM)

Mls		Sch.	m.	s.	Speed	m.	s.	Speed	m.	s.	Speed
0.0	MARGATE	0	0	00		0	00		0	00	
				pws	25						
3.2	Birchington		7	26	67	5	43	71	5	34	65
11.2	Herne Bay		15	25	48/71	13	20	51/74	13	52	42/68
14.8	Whitstable★		18	49	50/64	16	40	45/65	17	21	50/63
				sigs	20						
21.9	FAVERSHAM★	25	28	36	44/51	24	17	40/47	24	43	48/50
25.9	Teynham		33	06	74	29	07	70	29	21	68
29.2	SITTINGBOURNE	32½	35	55	53	31	58	52	32	18	
										sigs	40
32.3	Newington		39	01	71	35	05	68	35	49	57
										sigs	10
39.6	CHATHAM★	44	45	49	42	42	11	35	47	21	42
40.9	Rochester B. Jc.★		48	11	35	44	24	30	49	30	34
43.0	*Cuxton Rd S.B.*		51	37	35/40	48	34		52	57	40/31
47.0	Sole Street	57	57	59	35	57	06	26	60	12	31
53.4	Farningham Rd		63	50	84	63	36	81	66	14	83
				pws	15						
56.2	SWANLEY JUNC.	67	69	31		66	06	58	69	25	
				pws	22					pws	25
59.1	St Mary Cray		73	·34	62	68	42	72	73	33	61
							sigs	35			
61.6	*Bickley Junc.*	73	75	50	51	71	33	44	75	56	48
63.0	BROMLEY SOUTH		77	35	65	73	43	56	77	41	67
65.2	Beckenham Junc.★	78	80	20	40	76	46	32	80	21	42
69.9	HERNE HILL★	85	86	29	35	82	54	30	86	01	36
				pws	20						
73.9	VICTORIA	92	93	41		90	11		92	48	

Estimated net time (mins)	83¾	89¼	86

★Speed restriction

Ramsgate to Victoria via Chatham – contrasted rather sharply with the Folkestone route in that it had several permanent speed restrictions, numerous curves and was of an undulating character as well as having an awkward ascent of the North Downs from the east. The up journey provides the greater interest and in table 3 there are three runs of Mr A. J. Baker's timing. Early checks put the first of these three trains behind schedule; despite time being saved on the climb up Sole Street bank followed by 84 mph in the Farningham Road dip, relaying delays in the Swanley area proved too much of a handicap for a punctual arrival to be made in London. In detail B no. 916 fared very much better than had no. 921 and by Chatham had time in hand so much so that a not very energetic climb was indulged in to Sole Street. Even so an early arrival was made in London. The third of these runs features no. 914 fitted with the Lemaitre exhaust hauling a ten-coach train. A good start with close adherence to the schedule was spoiled with signal checks between Sittingbourne and Chatham and, notwithstanding a reasonable climb past Cuxton Road, little time was regained before another restriction was met with at Swanley. A fast run into the terminus was not sufficient for all the dropped minutes to be entirely recouped.

The Hastings via Battle route has its main interest south of Tonbridge because the London–Tonbridge length is common to the Folkestone services. The first hurdle to be met with after the permanent speed restriction on the approach to Tonbridge station is the 1 in 53 climbing curve to Somerhill Tunnel after which it is all against the grade (about 1 in 100) to Tunbridge Wells. Between there and Wadhurst there are three summits and two dips followed by a long downhill stretch as far as Robertsbridge, where the climb to Mountfield Tunnel starts. Two miles downhill from the tunnel precede a climb to Battle and a fall to Crowhurst. The ruling gradient between Tunbridge Wells and Hastings is 1 in 100.

Detail A of table 4 records no. 906 with a moderate load taking about 38½ minutes net to pass Tonbridge and then gradually improving on the booked time through to the first stop at Crowhurst covering the 28 miles in 39 minutes, so knocking a minute off schedule. With such a load the engine could hardly be said to have been extended. Rather more energetic is the same engine's run with the Saturday 3.25 pm from Charing Cross, timed by Mr Norman Harvey, on a heavy load. After a slowish start no. 906 was quicker throughout in detail B than on the first run. An up journey logged by Mr R. A. H. Weight (but not tabulated) of no. 908 hauling eleven coaches (357/380 tons) – the normal maximum loading for the route – non-stop between Crowhurst and Tunbridge Wells Central to a 35-minute schedule for the 23.3 miles is worthy of remark. Speeds were 67 mph after Battle, 45 mph at Mountfield and 67 mph again at Robertsbridge; the 10.2 miles to pass Etchingham took 13 minutes 51 seconds. Ticehurst Road was passed at 47 mph in 17 minutes 33 seconds and with a minimum of 36 mph Wadhurst was cleared in 24 minutes 25 seconds (a 2½-minute gain on the 27 minute booking) for the stop to be made in Tunbridge Wells in 31 minutes 21 seconds. This excellent work, especially the 10.4 mile climb to Wadhurst in 12 minutes 28 seconds, illustrates the competency of the class on this their traditional route.

Proceeding on to London there are two runs in table 5 of which that in detail A, with no. 922, was also timed by Mr Weight. No. 922 with a full loading forged ahead of schedule throughout and consequently paid the penalty in the suburban area. The other run, with no. 905, is extracted from the *Railway Magazine* and was made in 1931 or 1932 unusually loaded to twelve vehicles instead of the customary eleven. Even with no details of speeds available it is evident that a very good climb was made to Sevenoaks and another permanent way check did not prevent the City businessmen arriving virtually on time at Cannon Street.

Initially split between Deal and Eastbourne sheds the performance of the class was studied on the Eastern Section but failed to come under examination, or even notice, in the railway press so far as Central Section running was concerned, nor was the situation altered when members of the second batch were allocated to Eastbourne. Fortunately for posterity one recorder, the late H. T. Clements, did register the

Table 4. CHARING CROSS – CROWHURST

Detail		A			B		
Date		—			14 Aug. 1937		
Locomotive no.		906			906		
Vehicles		8			11		
Tare load (tons)		261			368		
Gross load (tons)		275			392		
Mls		Sch.	m.	s.	Sch.	m.	s.
0.0	CHARING CROSS	0	0	00			
			sigs				
1.9	LONDON BRIDGE★	5	5	15			
			sigs				
4.9	New Cross	9	10	00			
7.2	Hither Green	12	12	44			
11.2	Chislehurst	18	18	47			
13.8	ORPINGTON	21	22	12			
16.6	Knockholt		25	43			
20.6	Dunton Green		30	03			
22.1	SEVENOAKS T.H.	31	31	32			
27.0	Hildenborough		36	23			
29.5	TONBRIDGE★	39	39	19			
32.9	High Brooms★		46	00			
34.4	TUNBRIDGE WELLS C. ★	49	48	51	0	0	00
36.7	Frant		52	54		5	58
39.3	Wadhurst★		56	28		9	15
43.9	Ticehurst Road		62	11		14	22
47.5	Etchingham	66	65	22	18	17	36
49.6	Robertsbridge		67	24		19	36
55.6	Battle	75½	74	53	28	26	44
57.7	CROWHURST★	79	78	13	33	30	02
Estimated net time (mins)			77½			30	

★Speed restriction

Table 5. TUNBRIDGE WELLS CENTRAL – CANNON STREET

Detail		A				B		
Locomotive no.		922				905		
Vehicles		11				12		
Tare load (tons)		357				379		
Gross load (tons)		375				400		

Mls		Sch.	m.	s.	Speed	Sch.	m.	s.
0.0	TUNBRIDGE WELLS C.	0	0	00		0	0	00
1.5	High Brooms★		3	58			pws	
4.9	TONBRIDGE★	8	7	58	30	8	8	38
7.4	Hildenborough		11	43	37		12	32
9.3	*Weald Signal Box*		15	10	32			
11.7	*Sevenoaks Tunnel N.*		—		34		19	28
12.3	SEVENOAKS T.H.	21	20	27		20½	20	14
13.9	Dunton Green		22	11	58		—	
17.9	Knockholt		26	56	42	27½	26	57
20.6	ORPINGTON	31	29	42		30	—	
23.2	Chislehurst	33½	32	05	69	32½	—	
25.4	Grove Park		—		75		33	31
27.2	Hither Green	37	35	38		36	sigs	
			sigs					
29.6	New Cross	40	40	49		39	38	00
			sigs				pws	
32.6	LONDON BRIDGE★	44½ pass	46	05 pass		44	43	36
33.3	CANNON STREET	To Charing Cross				46	46	15

★Speed restriction

running on his visits into Sussex, some of the results of which are contained in tables 6 and 7. The first of these two tables deals with down runs of varying loadings; only no. 916 in detail B got a clear start to East Croydon and in consequence was able to improve on schedule. Thereafter it got a nasty relaying check on the racing ground through Horley, the effect of which could not be entirely nullified by the time Haywards Heath was reached. No. 915 with the lightest load (detail A) was obviously enjoying making up time dropped to East Croydon and for its driver's pains suffered a check outside Haywards Heath, while no. 913 on the eleven-coach train had too much of a handicap with the dead stand at Coulsdon and, despite fast running, lost six minutes because of it.

The up trains (table 7) had their difficulties too, especially no. 914 in detail A on the Lewes–East Croydon non-stop which did well in the disheartening circumstances. No. 910 was doubtless running well up to time and the checks were possibly of its own making but no. 902 got a beast of a permanent way slowing at Horley which gave no chance of a punctual arrival at Croydon. Central Section running, therefore, would appear to have been very much a subject for the connoisseur of locomotive performance.

The Schools first performed regularly on the

Table 6. VICTORIA – HAYWARDS HEATH

Detail		A			B			C	
Date		18 Oct. 1933			13 May 1934			24 Sept. 1933	
Train		9.10 pm			8.40 pm			8.40 pm	
Locomotive no.		915			916			913	
Vehicles		7			10			11	
Tare load (tons)		220			270			350	
Gross load (tons)		235			290			370	

Mls		Sch.	m.	s.	Speed	m.	s.	Speed	m.	s.	Speed
0.0	VICTORIA	0	0	00		0	00		0	00	
			sigs								
2.7	Clapham Junction		7	05		5	45		6	50	
									pws		
10.6	EAST CROYDON	17	18	45		16	00		19	55	
0.9	South Croydon		2	40		2	55		3	20	
3.0	Purley		5	50	46	6	15	44	6	50	40
4.5	Coulsdon North★	8	7	55	25	—		30	sig. stop		
8.3	*Quarry S.B.*		13	50	39	14	40	35	20	20	29
11.3	Earlswood	17	16	50		18	25	60	24	20	
						pws		40			
15.5	Horley		20	20	73	24	05	60	28	00	71
19.0	Three Bridges	25	23	40		27	50		31	25	
21.4	*Balcombe T.S.B.*		26	10	52	30	35	49	34	10	47
23.6	Balcombe		28	40	64	33	00	68	36	40	67
			sigs								
27.5	HAYWARDS HEATH	35	35	30		37	05		41	05	
Estimated net time (mins)			33¼			34			34¼		

★Speed restriction

Western Section when nos 924 to 933 were sent straight from construction to Fratton shed to work the Portsmouth Direct services. Just over 73½ miles from Waterloo, the naval town had to be reached by the fast trains in an hour and a half which allowed for speed restrictions at Woking, Guildford and Havant and, with a clear road, presented no problem. More often than not, however, there were permanent way checks to be absorbed (some of these could be quite awkward on the climbs between Guildford and Havant) and traffic delays. These latter were at their worst between Havant and Portsmouth and, in the up direction, on the approach to Woking.

Anyhow, table 8 opens with a completely unchecked run on the 6.50 pm from Waterloo to Havant, allowed 82 minutes for the 66½ miles. No. 928 with ten coaches soon got a minute in hand but inexplicably lost it and more beside between Woking and Guildford and then made heavy weather of the climb from Witley to Haslemere falling to 23 mph in the process. Free running down through Liss recouped the loss

Table 7. LEWES – EAST CROYDON

Detail		A				B				C		
Date		5 May 1933				26 Apr. 1935				28 May 1935		
Train		6.53 pm				1.14 pm				1.14 pm		
Locomotive no.		914				910				902		
Vehicles		7				8				10		
Tare load (tons)		220				265				315		
Gross load (tons)		235				285				335		
Mls		Sch.	m.	s.	Speed	Sch.	m.	s.	Speed	m.	s.	Speed
0.0	LEWES	0	0	00								
9.3	Wivelsfield		14	00	30							
				sigs								
12.2	HAYWARDS HEATH	19	18	40	30	0	0	00		0	00	
16.1	Balcombe		23	25	50		6	40	47	6	50	48
18.3	*Balcombe T.S.B.*		26	00	50		9	20		9	36	48
20.7	Three Bridges	29	28	20		12	11	50		12	00	70
				pws	40						pws	
24.2	Horley		32	55	60		14	55	70	14	50	10
28.4	Earlswood	37	37	10	55	20	18	50		24	20	43
				sigs								
31.5	*Quarry S.B.*		40	50	40		22	10	50	28	20	55
								sigs				
35.2	Coulsdon North	45		—		28	26	55	30	33	40	30
								sigs				
36.7	Purley		46	55	70		29	05	30	35	40	60
				sigs								
38.8	South Croydon		51	20			32	00		37	50	
39.7	EAST CROYDON	51	53	15		34	33	40		39	55	
Estimated net time (mins)		46				31½				34		

and eventually Havant was reached with two minutes exactly to spare. No. 931, in detail B, was also heading ten vehicles on the 6.50 pm but on a Sunday when it was non-stop to Fratton in 89 minutes. A dead stand for signals and a permanent way check made the train nearly ten minutes late in the first dozen miles so that, on passing Hampton Court Junction, there was no more than 62¾ minutes available for 59½ miles and another relaying check to be encountered. Who would have ventured that the train would be over two minutes early at Fratton? Yet that is what happened on this extraordinary run. Speed was 69 mph at Byfleet; the 30 mph permanent restriction at Guildford was observed in true Nelsonian fashion, followed by a fine 36 mph up to Haslemere and with almost 80 mph at Liss and an excellent 54 mph on the climb to Buriton, the schedule was bettered. By contrast no. 933, with one coach more on the 11.50 am, could not make up all the loss of an early slowing and arrived in Portsmouth half-a-minute in arrears.

This same engine, in the capable hands of

Table 8. WATERLOO – PORTSMOUTH & SOUTHSEA

	A	B	C	Detail		D	E
Locomotive no.	928	931	933			933	926
Vehicles	10	10	11			10	11
Tare load (tons)	324	324	356			324	356
Gross load (tons)	345	345	385			345	385

Mls	Sch. (stop)	m. s.	Spd	m. s.	Spd	m. s.	Spd	Detail	Mls	Sch.	m. s.	m. s.
0.0	0	0 00		0 00		0 00		WATERLOO	73.6	90	85 12	107 26
												sig. stop
3.9	7	6 55		sig. stop		7 49		Clapham Junc.★	69.7	83	78 56	91 58
						pws					sigs	sig. stop
7.2		10 35		15 32		12 47		Wimbledon	66.4		75 32	81 12
				pws	15							
12.0		15 20		24 13		17 54		Surbiton	61.6		71 34	73 43
												sigs
13.3	17½	16 35		26 11		19 08	67	*Hampton C. Jc.*	60.3	73½	70 28	72 29
17.1		20 10		30 10		22 29		Walton/Weyb'ge	54.5		65 47	67 24
21.7		24 10		34 28	69	26 38	68	Byfleet	51.9		64 36	65 03
24.3	28½	27 35		36 55	38	29 16	35	WOKING★	49.3	62½	60 41	62 21
											sigs	
26.8		31 45		39 50	63	32 35	61	Worplesdon	46.8		55 52	59 19
30.3	36	36 50	30	43 19		36 52	28	GUILDFORD★	43.3	55	50 56	53 54
												sigs
34.5		43 00	60	47 48	65	42 32	58	Godalming	39.1		46 09	48 36
36.3		45 15		49 30		44 40		Milford	37.3		44 33	46 58
38.5		48 00	41	51 48	54	47 44	34	Witley	35.1		42 33	45 01
43.0	54½	55 30	23	57 20	36	56 19	22	HASLEMERE	30.6	41	38 03	40 17
46.9		59 15		60 42		60 15		Liphook	26.8		33 39	35 51
51.5		63 35	74	64 26	79	64 22	71	Liss	22.1		28 27	30 13
54.9	67	66 45		67 10	73	68 11		PETERSFIELD	18.7	27½	25 39	27 14
57.3		69 35	51	69 20	54	71 21	37	*Buriton Sdg S.B.*	16.4		23 19	24 54
63.3	77½	75 30	62	75 04	74	78 18	67	Rowlands Cas.★	10.4		13 56	15 17
66.5	81 (82)	80 00		78 49		81 42		HAVANT★	7.1	9½	9 35	10 28
				pws	22	—	63				pws	pws
72.8	88 (89)			86 43		88 37		FRATTON	0.8		2 04	2 14
73.6	90					90 33		P'MOUTH & S.	0.0	0	0 00	0 00

Estimated net time (mins) 75¾ 89   82 87

★Speed restriction

Schedule times given for Woking are in fact for the Junction

51

22. No. 915 'Brighton' approaching Wivelsfield with a down Eastbourne Pullman car train.

driver Stares, did very much better on the first of the up runs as detail D demonstrates. This was the 12 noon departure from Portsmouth on 4 June 1937 which Rev. R. S. Haines (the recorder of both up runs in this table) noted as leaving three minutes late. So brisk was the running that a relaying delay beyond Fratton was speedily wiped out and with fine climbing up from Rowlands Castle and again to Haslemere driver Stares had the train right on schedule by Haslemere and picked up another minute on to Guildford. Woking, of course, had to be negotiated at slow speed but even with a further signal check at Earlsfield an early arrival was not to be denied to this enterprising driver. Last of all is no. 926 on the eleven-coach 9.57 am train with driver Stanford in charge. By dint of good climbing the early deficit was wiped out and

even Woking was passed without hindrance. With a minute in hand at Hampton Court Junction an early arrival was very much on the cards until a whole series of signal checks completely ruined the conclusion of a competent run.

Before leaving the Portsmouth route reference may be made to some of the semi-fast trains. The Saturday 6.50 pm from Waterloo called at Guildford and Havant and was allowed 51 minutes for the 36¼ miles. Not surprisingly this, with a clear road, was more than enough as Rev. Haines's records indicate: in May 1937 no. 930 with ten vehicles was through Haslemere in 18 minutes 18 seconds, Petersfield in 31 minutes 12 seconds to stop in Havant in 46 minutes 26 seconds, whereas no. 932 with one coach more took 19 minutes 51 seconds to Haslemere, 31 minutes 27 seconds to Petersfield and beat no. 930's time to Havant by eight seconds. Efforts to obtain even-time running were

23. No. 927 'Clifton' passes Petersfield with the 3.50 pm Waterloo–Portsmouth Harbour service on 10 June 1937 just before the class was ousted from the route by electrification.

occasionally made and on 29 June 1937 Fratton's spare engine, no. 927, with driver May of Fratton, got mighty close. Loaded to eight coaches (about 260 tons full) the 5.50 pm from Waterloo restarted from the Haslemere stop to pass Liphook in 4 minutes 54 seconds, Liss in 8 minutes 42 seconds (probably touching 90 mph in the process), Petersfield in 11 minutes 23 seconds, Buriton signal box in 13 minutes 34 seconds, Rowlands Castle in 19 minutes 36 seconds and stopped in Havant in 23 minutes 28 seconds for the 23 miles 36 chains. Rev. Haines did not claim slight signals approaching Havant; but F. E. Box, who was also recording no. 927's progress did and he reckoned that, if a clear run-in had been made, the vital second would have been saved!

Paradoxically the Portsmouth electrification had the ultimate effect of enhancing the reputation of the Schools rather than to lessen the opportunities for the class to demonstrate its prowess. As mentioned in chapter 2 the ten members of the class based at Fratton were transferred to Bournemouth shed and, after the footplatemen there had become used to the type, began to demonstrate not only an equality with but even a superiority to the King Arthurs, which they had displaced, and – tell it not in Gath! – also the Lord Nelsons.

The sole non-stop train between London and Bournemouth was the 'Bournemouth Limited' (4.30 pm from Waterloo and 8.40 am up from Bournemouth Central), allowed 116 minutes in the down direction and two more minutes on the up run; on these turns, of which the load limit was laid down as 365 tons (in effect eleven coaches), the class soon established itself. Table 9 embraces two down and three up journeys. In detail A no. 928 had the advantage of a train not loaded to the limit (a winter loading, for this

53

was 23 March 1938) and passed the summit at milepost 31 at 63 mph – an excellent figure for the down direction – and sped on to Basingstoke in the middle seventies so that the arrears of the permanent way check at Malden were soon recouped and more beside. A speed of 85 mph was attained near Shawford before the inevitable signal checks were met with in the Southampton area because the train was running before time in an attempt to offset a further relaying slack near Sway. With 74 mph before Brockenhurst and 77 mph down Hinton Admiral bank, driver Oliver's attempt at an on-time arrival was just thwarted by a signal check outside Bournemouth Central. Net time for the 108 miles works out at no more than 109 minutes. The other down run (detail B) is of no. 930 overloaded by one coach and in the hands of driver Baker. Apart from signals approaching Redbridge this combination had the luxury of an unchecked run and demonstrated that an extra coach posed no great problem in keeping – or, in this case, improving upon – the 55 mph schedule. These two runs have the fastest net and actual times respectively for the down 'Bournemouth Limited' that can be traced.

The first of the up runs (detail C of this same table) had a handicap of a string of relaying checks so that no. 931, even with a winter loading, was nearly seven minutes late on passing Eastleigh. A splendid climb, for 345 tons, was made to Litchfield and beyond Basingstoke speed reached 80 mph before there was another slack near Pirbright Junction. Driver Peterson never gave up but could not prevent a late arrival of 1½ minutes; the net time did not exceed 108 minutes – 60 mph for the start-to-stop journey. Two runs recorded by Doctor Fluker (who also was the recorder of the two down runs in this table) follow. Both these very competent runs feature no. 929 and driver Peterson, one with the maximum loading and the other

with one coach in excess of it. The first, despite a bad signal check on the approach to Worting Junction and relaying work at Earlsfield, just scraped into Waterloo on time having reached 85 mph before and 81 mph after Weybridge, while the second had the scales weighed too heavily against it with three permanent way slacks to contend with to be able to arrive at the terminus at the advertised time.

Excellent as the work with the daily non-stop Bournemouth service was, it was the work with the Waterloo–Southampton Central non-stops that really compels the greater admiration. Here, in table 10, are the three finest of the fifteen down runs the author has at his disposal, none of which had a load of less than twelve coaches (the 400-ton limit laid down for these trains) and of which only one had a net time exceeding the schedule, and even in that case by no more than thirty seconds! The first run suffered a long stand for signals in the outer suburbs from which recovery, if at first a little cautious, soon became very marked. The deficit shrank to 7½ minutes by Worting Junction the train arriving at Southampton 4¾ minutes late after a delay which had cost eleven minutes. In detail B no. 931 had a fourteen-coach train with the disadvantage of a permanent way slack on the racing ground down to Winchester. Driver Billett made a nicely judged run to arrive in Southampton right on time. In detail C no. 932 reappears with no less than fifteen coaches (more than 100 tons overloaded) and, enjoying an unhindered run, got into Southampton with 2½ minutes to spare.

Space precludes tabulation of semi-fast trains – nonetheless at least one example of how the class dealt with that type of traffic must be given. On 18 August 1938 Mr H. T. Clements found no. 930 on the 8.30 am from Waterloo loaded up to fourteen vehicles (five of which were for boat traffic to be detached at

Table 9. 'BOURNEMOUTH LIMITED'

	A	B	Detail	C	D	E
Loco. no.	928	930		931	929	929
Vehicles	10	12		10	11	12
Tare load (tons)	321	384		323	352	386
Gross load (tons)	345	410		345	375	415

Mls	Sch.	m. s.	Spd	m. s.	Spd		Mls	Sch.	m. s.	Spd	m. s.	Spd	m. s.	Spd
0.0	0	0 00		0 00		WATERLOO	108.0	118	119 26		117 56		122 24	
3.9	7	7 00		7 26		Clapham Jc.★	104.1	111	113 20	35	111 56	36	116 45	
											pws			
7.2		10 56		11 19		Wimbledon	100.8		110 15	67	105 26	72	113 16	
		pws	20										pws	
12.0		17 37		16 03		Surbiton	96.0		106 05	69	101 37	76	106 10	70
19.1	28	24 46		22 36	58	Weybridge	88.9		100 18	78	96 05	78	100 24	75
24.3		29 16		27 29		WOKING	83.7	92	96 02	66	92 15		96 28	81
28.0		32 33		31 21		Brookwood	80.0		pws	20	—			
31.0		35 21	63	34 40	54	*Milepost 31*	77.0		87 46	71	86 58	70	91 16	70
36.5		40 05	75	40 01		Fleet	71.5		83 20	78	82 20	76	86 44	74
42.2		44 48	76	45 12	69	Hook	65.8		78 53	80	77 42	76	82 04	75
47.8		49 25		50 13		BASINGSTOKE	59.2		74 35	75	73 05		77 32	
50.3	54	51 44		52 47		*Worting Jc.*★	57.7	69	72 29	63	70 35		75 16	
											sigs			
—	—	—		—		*Litchfield S.B.*	51.8		66 37	54	60 52	49	68 56	46
58.1		60 12		60 43		Micheldever	49.9		64 41	55	58 35		66 35	
66.6		67 10		67 11		WINCHESTER	41.4		55 14	53	48 41		55 06	
69.7		—	85	—	87	Shawford	38.3		51 50	56	45 03	55	52 17	
73.6	75½	72 20	63	72 12		EASTLEIGH	34.4	41	47 52	59	40 42		47 49	54
78.2	80½	77 15		76 27		*Northam Jc.*★	29.8	35	41 32	18	33 32		40 55	
79.2		79 26		78 17		SO'TON CEN.	28.8		39 31	55	31 30		38 28	
		sigs		sigs									pws	
81.8		83 56	20	82 35		Redbridge★	24.2		36 13	40	28 20		32 15	
		sigs									pws			
85.4		90 35	47	89 11		Lyndhurst Rd	22.6		27 15	15	24 22		28 52	
											pws			
88.0		93 26	61	92 26	54	Beaulieu Rd	20.0		24 44	68	22 06	76	26 16	
92.8		97 35	74	97 07	66	BROCKENHURST	15.2		20 46	75	18 06		21 41	64
		pws	20											
95.5		102 20		100 04	51	Sway	12.5		18 09	56	15 35		17 26	
										pws			pws	
101.0		108 30	77	105 22	74	Hinton Admiral	7.0		10 16	52	9 51	50	11 00	45
104.3		111 15		108 07		Christchurch★	3.7		6 38	53	6 28	64	6 59	
		sigs												
108.0	116	117 00		112 56		B'MOUTH CEN.	0.0	0	0 00		0 00		0 00	

Estimated net time (mins)	109	110½				108	110½	114½

★Speed restriction

Schedule times given for Woking are in fact for the Junction

Table 10. WATERLOO – SOUTHAMPTON CENTRAL

		A		B		C	Detail			D		E	
		4 Aug. 1938		—		2 Sep. 1938	Date			19 Aug. 1939		14 Oct. 1938	
		12.30 pm		—		6.30 pm	Train			7.20 pm		3.20 pm	
		932		931		932	Locomotive no.			930		933	
		12		14		15	Vehicles			12		14	
		385		454		490	Tare load (tons)			385		453	
		410		480		525	Gross load (tons)			410		485	
Mls	Sch.	m. s.	Spd	m. s.	Spd	m. s.		Mls	Sch.	m. s.	Spd	m. s.	Spd
0.0	0	0 00		0 00		0 00	WATERLOO	79.2	90	94 25 sigs		86 50	
3.9	7	7 35		7 08		6 51	Clapham Jc.★	75.4	83	86 25	45	80 20	40
7.2		11 50 sig. stop		11 16		11 05	Wimbledon	72.0		82 10		76 50	62
12.0		25 10		16 15		17 04	Surbiton	67.2		75 30	20	72 10	62
13.3	18	—		17 33	65	—	Hampton C. Jc.	65.9	73½	sigs		—	
19.1		33 55	53	23 08	59	24 22	Weybridge	60.1		65 50	75	66 05	68
21.7		36 30		—	65	—	Byfleet	57.5		63 55	81	64 05	76
24.3	29	39 05		28 26		29 30	WOKING	54.9	63	، 61 55		62 00	
28.0		43 00		32 34		33 45	Brookwood	51.2		59 10	75	59 00	
31.0		46 20	53	36 11	48	37 20	Milepost 31	48.2		—	65	—	64
36.5		51 40	66	41 55		42 52	Fleet	42.8		51 55	69	51 45	70
39.8		54 40		—		—	Winchfield	39.5		49 05		49 00	
42.2		56 50	60	47 40	62	49 01	Hook	37.1		47 05	72	47 00	65
47.8	54	61 50		53 15		53 57	BASINGSTOKE	31.4	42	42 20	65	42 20	
50.3	57	64 30	47	56 01	51	57 12	Worting Jc.★	29.0	39½	39 50 sigs	20	40 00	55
56.3		—		62 43		—	Litchfield S.B.	22.9		—		—	
58.1		72 50		—		65 54	Micheldever	21.1		28 35	50	30 50	44
61.8		—		67 46 pws	75	—	Wallers A.S.B.	17.4		—		—	
66.6		79 30	79	74 04		73 00	WINCHESTER	12.7		18 40	50	19 30	44
69.7		81 50	80	77 24		75 15	Shawford	9.5		14 55	50	15 20	47
73.6	79½	84 50	60	80 46		78 10	EASTLEIGH	5.7	10	10 25	47	10 40	42
77.3		88 20		83 51		81 12	St Denys	1.9		5 25		5 20	
78.2	84½	89 45		84 59		82 37	Northam Jc.★	1.1	3½	—		—	
79.2	87½	92 15		87 24		85 05	SO'TON CEN.	0.0	0	0 00		0 00	
		81¼		84		85	Estimated net time (mins)			85½		86¾	

★Speed restriction

Schedule times given for Woking are in fact for the Junction

Southampton) giving a tare load of 443 tons or about 475 tons full. Surbiton was reached in 17 minutes 40 seconds and the next lap to Woking took 16 minutes exactly start-to-stop. Restarting from Woking the milepost 31 summit was cleared at 45 mph in 12 minutes precisely and, with a maximum of 61 mph, the 23.4 miles to the Basingstoke stop were completed in 29 minutes 40 seconds. Speed, no higher than 33 mph at Worting Junction, rose to 78 mph on the descent to Winchester, reached in 24 minutes 20 seconds; with 70 mph through Eastleigh the last leg to Southampton took 15 minutes 40 seconds, which was most satisfactory work with such a load, bettering the Waterloo–Southampton schedule by no less than 6 minutes 40 seconds.

Two runs demonstrate work with up trains. No. 930 (detail D) made an excellent sustained climb up the bank from Winchester and it is a pity that the recorder did not note the time at the summit. Even so, it would be surprising if 50 mph was not sustained all the way up. After this excellent climb it was poor reward for the run to be spoiled by signal checks in the suburban area of London. The other up run, with no. 933, had the bonus of unimpeded progress which was just as well considering the fourteen-coach load scaled not far short of 500 tons. A steady 44 mph was maintained up the bank through Micheldever and beyond Worting Junction the close correspondence in passing times with the previous run will be observed. Apart from details B and C, which were recorded by Mr R. E. Charlewood and the author respectively, the runs in this table are from the notebook of Mr H. T. Clements.

The 36-minute schedule for the 28.8 miles from Southampton to Bournemouth might not appear on the face of things too strenuous and it certainly was not for moderately loaded trains, but when it came to loads in excess of 400 tons it

was fairly exacting in view of the curvature encountered in the early part of the run, Sway bank (which with luck might be rushed) and the grind up to Pokesdown after the restriction at Christchurch. Detail A in table 11 has no. 932 with thirteen coaches on the 12.30 pm from Waterloo on 11 August 1938 falling to 46 mph on Sway bank but nonetheless arriving at Bournemouth with half-a-minute in hand. No. 925·heading fourteen vehicles even improved on no. 932's times until the permanent way check before Christchurch made the ascent to Bournemouth a rather laboured affair. The author had the same engine on a fifteen-coach 525-ton gross load which, although not so swift as this, did pass Sway in 21 minutes 47 seconds before relaying and signal checks intervened – net time would have been about 35¼ minutes. No. 930, on the 8.30 am from Waterloo previously mentioned, with its load reduced to nine coaches (290 tons tare, 320 tons gross) ran to Brockenhurst in 17½ minutes with a maximum speed of 60 mph and then went on to Bournemouth in 19¾ minutes with speeds of 36 mph on Sway bank and a maximum of 72 mph before Christchurch.

In the up direction no. 931 was timed by Mr D. S. M. Barrie on 23 July 1938 with a nine-coach train (261 tons tare, 275 tons gross): Christchurch was passed in 6 minutes 12 seconds, Hinton Admiral in 9 minutes 50 seconds, New Milton in 12 minutes 52 seconds and Lymington Junction in 17¾ minutes exactly. Speeds were 68 mph before Christchurch, 45 mph minimum up Hinton Admiral bank and 67 mph coming down from Sway. After Brockenhurst the engine was not pressed and came to a halt at Southampton Central in 33 minutes 46 seconds. In table 11 detail C no. 930 on 19 August 1939 performed very well with the twelve-coach 6.40 pm departure from Bournemouth. Going up the scale to thirteen-

Table 11. SOUTHAMPTON CENTRAL – BOURNEMOUTH CENTRAL

A	B	Detail	C	D	E
932	925	Locomotive no.	930	929 (L)	930
13	14	Vehicles	12	13	14
417	455	Tare load (tons)	385	420	447
445	485	Gross load (tons)	410	470	480
H. T. Clements	S. W. Corbett	Recorder	H. T. Clements	Dr Fluker	H. T. Clements

Mls	Sch	m. s.	Spd	m. s.	Spd		Mls	Sch	m. s.	Spd	m. s.	Spd	m. s.	Spd
0.0	0	0 00		0 00		SOUTHAMPTON C.	28.8	36	34 10		35 15 sigs		34 40	
2.6		6 05	40	5 56	35	Redbridge★	26.2		29 20		30 05		30 30	
6.2		10 55	42	10 39	48	Lyndhurst Road	22.6		25 50	68	25 55	70	27 00	70
8.8		14 10	48	13 37	56	Beaulieu Road	20.0		22 45	56	23 28	62	24 35	62
13.6		18 56	64	18 10	65	BROCKENHURST★	15.2		18 20	64	19 13		19 55	65
16.3		22 00	46	21 12	55	Sway	12.5		15 35	62	16 37	69	17 10	56
19.3		25 05		29 16	62	New Milton	9.5		12 35	51	—		13 50	43
21.8		27 25	72	26 38 pws	72	Hinton Admiral	7.0		9 50		10 42	48	10 40	
25.1		30 25	53	29 51	20	Christchurch★	3.7		6 35	64	7 01	62	7 00	62
27.6		33 40	37	—		Boscombe	1.2		—		—		—	
28.8	36	35 25		38 06		BOURNEMOUTH C.	0.0	0	0 00		0 00		0 00	
		35½		35		Estimated net time (mins)			34¼		34½		34¾	

★Speed restriction

coach trains no. 929 fitted with Lemaitre exhaust figures in detail D. No apparent advantage due to this fitment can be discerned from the figures. Finally in this table no. 930 reappears with a fourteen-coach load on the 6.40 pm on 23 September 1938 which taxed the engine on the climb up to New Milton. After Brockenhurst a very determined effort was made so much so that this run finished no more than thirty seconds behind the twelve-coach example.

This account of running between London and Bournemouth shows the Schools at the pinnacle of their performance and underlines the exceptionally good power/weight ratio which the design possessed. The main problem arose in accelerating from checks with trains exceeding 400 tons in weight which sometimes could prove a slow process, but once on the move running was lively. It has been propounded that the limited water supply of the tenders inhibited full exploitation of the class on the Western Section but this overlooks the fact that there was only one train that could do that – the once-a-day 'Bournemouth Limited'. It was curious, of course, that duty did fall to be worked by the Schools. All other trains called at Southampton where water could be taken and, even with the 'Limited', there were water columns awaiting parched engines at the buffer stops at Waterloo. Just where the engines were inhibited by this

24. No. 928 'Stowe' heading a down Bournemouth train on a summer Saturday past West Weybridge at the start of the climb to milepost 31.

C. R. L. Coles

reason anywhere on the Southern is difficult to imagine.

Inhibition, from whatever quarter it might have come, was certainly not present in the runs in table 12! Dorchester to Wareham once (in LSWR days) figured in a 15-minute schedule for the 14 miles 79 chains which was a pretty sporting proposition even if 22 yards short for an even-time booking. In the late 1930s there was a 16-minute schedule which produced some fun as witness detail A where driver Guy had no. 928 with four coaches and a challenge from the recorder to 'do Moreton to Wool in three minutes'. One hopes the recorder duly rewarded the effort because he did get the highest known speed – 95 mph – by a Schools and the driver was only three seconds beyond the target! In detail B no. 337 is not a mistake for no. 927 or no. 937 but arises from the author commenting in *Bulleid's Pacifics* 'whether or not T9 class 4–4–0 locomotives achieved the even time booking . . . . is not clear.' Mr Barrie kindly intimated that these game little engines were capable of doing so with details of a run he experienced in 1946 on his demobilisation leave. As he remarks, it '. . . gave me a slightly flattering (as it was to prove) view of post-war running in this country!' The fun runs of table 12 conclude with no. 924 bettering even time with a nine-coach train.

The class, prior to 1939, never had any regular duties taking its members to Salisbury, such visits as there were being isolated filling-in trips, or test runs using scheduled services for the

59

Table 12. DORCHESTER – WAREHAM

Detail		A			B			C		
Locomotive no.		928			337			924		
Vehicles		4			5			9		
Tare load (tons)		128			160			294		
Gross load (tons)		135			165			310		
Driver		Guy			—			Allen		
Recorder		Dr J. Fluker			D. S. M. Barrie			Dr J. Fluker		
Mls		Sch.	m.	s.	Speed	m.	s.	Speed	m.	s.	Speed
0.0	DORCHESTER	0	0	00		0	00		0	00	
5.6	Moreton		6	05	81	6	32	73	6	36	74
10.0	Wool		9	08	95	9	55	82	9	56	88
13.9	*Worgret Junction*★		11	45	43	13	08	62	—		
						sigs					
15.0	WAREHAM	16	13	45		15	03	†	14	38	

★Speed restriction   †Schedule 17 minutes

purpose; even so those that did occur merit some extended examination. When new no. 909 was tried out on the route with a train scaling just over 400 tons tare but for some reason it made a poor fist of its attempt to get up to London in the 90-minute schedule. There was a lack-lustre start and the arrival in Waterloo was nearly 6 minutes over schedule with a net time of 93¾ minutes.

Several years went by before the Bulleid modified engines put in an appearance – and then to some effect! First of all there is no. 931 with the standard Lemaitre multiple-jet exhaust and large-diameter chimney, in the hands of driver Silk of Nine Elms just before his retirement, on the Saturday 10.24 am departure from Waterloo (the first of five parts of the 'Atlantic Coast Express'). As will be seen from detail A of table 13 the load was no heavier than about 300 tons and, although one could wish for the data to be rather more detailed, it is clearly apparent that some exceptional running was being indulged in. Even-time must have been attained in the neighbourhood of milepost 31

and in an hour about 68 miles had been covered before the inevitable check on the approach to Salisbury was encountered.

The other down run tabulated took place in mid-week when a full load of 400 tons was tackled by driver Rice, also of Nine Elms shed, with no. 937, which had the non-standard Lemaitre exhaust and modified cylinders. The 355-ton limit for the 10.35 am was exceeded for the purpose of this test for which a member of the CME's department was on the footplate as an observer. A fast exit from London was slightly checked in the outer suburbs and then severely so at Woking which was passed at 24 mph. A fine recovery followed so that the summit at milepost 31 was breasted at all but 60 mph and an excellent piece of sustained running was then enjoyed until a peculiar isolated signal check was encountered on the approach to Whitchurch from which recovery was quick and with a swift downhill run into Salisbury a remarkable net time – for this load – of 80½ minutes resulted.

The last of the runs in table 13 is the return to

Table 13. 'ATLANTIC COAST EXPRESS'

	A	B	Detail	C
Date	July 1939	12 July 1939		12 July 1939
Locomotive no.	931 (L)	937 (L)		937 (L)
Vehicles	9	12		12
Tare load (tons)	288	388		387
Gross load (tons)	305	410		410

Mls	Sch.	m. s.	Sch.	m. s.	Spd		Mls	Sch.	m. s.	Spd
0.0	0	0 00	0	0 00		WATERLOO	83.7	86	80 55	
3.9	7	7 10	7	6 45		Clapham Junc.★	79.8	79	74 24	
				sigs						
7.2		10 55		11 15		Wimbledon	76.5		71 29	75
				sigs						
9.8		13 25		14 35		Malden	73.9		—	
12.0		15 20		16 52	62	Surbiton	71.7		67 46	78
13.3	18	—	17	18 08		*Hampton Ct. Jc.*	70.4		66 44	78
19.1		21 15		23 11	72	Weybridge	64.6		62 09	69
				sigs						
24.3	30	25 30	28	28 19	24	WOKING	59.4	60	55 19	stop
									sigs	
28.0		28 30		34 16		Brookwood	55.7		50 47	79
31.0		—		37 33	59	*Milepost 31*	52.7		—	
36.5		35 15		42 35	69	Fleet	47.2		43 56	76
39.8		37 45		45 26	67	Winchfield	43.9		41 24	77
42.2		39 35		47 32	69	Hook	41.5		39 34	84
47.8		43 50		52 14	68	BASINGSTOKE	35.9		35 31	81
50.3	56	—	54	55 01	52	*Worting Junc.*	33.4	37	33 41	78
52.4		48 00		57 21	60	Oakley	31.3		32 02	71
55.6		50 45		60 24	68	Overton	28.1		29 23	69
				sigs						
59.2		53 40		63 29	58	Whitchurch	24.5		26 19	72
61.1		55 00		65 17	70	Hurstbourne	22.6		24 43	73
66.4		58 45		69 25	84	ANDOVER JUNC.	17.3		20 36	84
72.7		64 00		74 32	60	Grateley	11.0		15 47	60
		sigs								
78.2		71 20		79 20	85	Porton	5.5		9 35	44
		sig. stop								
82.6	85½	—	83½	82 42		*Tunnel Junc.★*	1.1	3	3 32	
83.7	88	81 50	86	84 53		SALISBURY	0.0	0	0 00	
		74½		80½		Estimated net time (mins)			76¼	

★Speed restriction

Schedule times given for Woking are in fact for the Junction

25. No. 929 'Malvern', resplendent in Bournemouth green livery, leaving Weymouth with a four-coach train. It was on such light formations that the Dorchester drivers used to delight in giving their steed its head between Dorchester and Wareham.

London by no. 937 and driver Rice the same day on the 2.14 pm from Salisbury. This log, taken by Mr F. E. Box (as was the down run) leaves one rather breathless for, with 410 tons, Porton was passed at 44 mph, Andover Junction cleared in 20½ minutes, even-time attained between Worting Junction and Basingstoke after which speed rose into the eighties and still no. 937 forged ahead. A special stop had to be made at Woking to set down a party and so the 59.4 miles were covered in 55¼ minutes. For the purpose of the table running times are given without any deduction for the standing period at Woking. With as lively work east of Woking as there had been to the west and no checks, the 'Atlantic Coast Express' came to rest at Waterloo in just under 81 minutes from Salisbury *inclusive* of stopping and restarting at Woking! This throws up a phenomenal net time of 76¼ minutes, which would have been considered very good for a rebuilt Merchant Navy engine twenty-five years later; the power output from Porton to Grateley may be calculated as 1130 EDHP (representing 1380 IHP) and from Andover to Oakley not far short of 1500 IHP. Nothing more needs to be added on the finest-ever recorded high-speed run by a Schools with a 400-ton load. Sadly it was not to happen again.

5
Wartime

War brought no immediate dramatic changes for the Schools. For the first three months, apart from anti-glare screens being fitted between cab and tender and the deceleration of services, there was little change and certainly none in the continuation of technical improvements. Engines were still being equipped with the multiple-jet exhaust and large-diameter chimney and turned out in the new style of lettering in one or other of the shades of green. The 'Bournemouth Limited', although stripped of its name, functioned to a slower schedule; elsewhere, after the initial cancellations in favour of evacuation specials and the like, the trains the Schools held as their preserve continued even if to less exacting timings. A couple of appearances of the class (nos 928 and 933) at Blandford in November 1939, doubtless on troop trains worked in from the Broadstone direction, were reported indicating a short extension of the range of the class.

Early in 1940 the Lord Nelsons were all gathered into Nine Elms for work on the Western Section. This again had no immediate effect on nos 924 to 933 at Bournemouth although the Nelsons did frequent the route more on duties worked by Nine Elms. Then in the spring of 1940 the stalemate between the opposing warring sides was suddenly broken. The retreat to Dunkirk and the evacuation which followed caused some of the Schools class to find themselves in strange parts of the

Southern. On 7 June 1940 no. 928 was noted leaving Exeter Central with an up train of empty stock while no. 930 took the 12.50 pm to Waterloo as far as Salisbury returning with the 2.50 pm ex Waterloo from Salisbury piloted by T9 class no. 729. Ten days later no. 918 was observed also at Exeter Central on an up empty stock train.

With the country attempting to turn itself into an island fortress the need for the Flaman recorders declined and the equipment was removed from those engines fitted with it. The necessity to retain a dozen of the class at St Leonards lessened and so, after Dunkirk, five were moved away – nos 900, 901 and 903 to Stewarts Lane (as well as nos 912 and 918 from Ramsgate) and nos 908 and 909 to Bricklayers Arms. This in theory minimised the danger of being subject to aerial damage or engulfed by invading forces, but in effect brought the locomotives into rather more direct danger when the sustained night bombing of London began in the autumn of 1940.

At the end of the year, in December, no. 921 became the subject of experiment with the Stokes automatic drifting valve, instead of the standard pressure relief valves, in an effort to overcome the disadvantages of the admitted cold air causing flaws to develop in the superheater elements and oxidisation of hot oil in the cylinders. The drifting valve, designed to pass a small amount of steam to the cylinders when the

26. When no. 852 'Sir Walter Raleigh' sustained a direct hit at Nine Elms shed on the night of 16/17 April 1941, no. 927 'Clifton' was standing on the adjacent track and received more than superficial damage, as the scene the morning after indicates.

engine was running with the regulator shut to prevent a vacuum arising in the cylinders, only operated when the engine was moving (by means of a vacuum pump actuated from the inside expansion link); a control valve operated by steam pressure in the steam chest ensured the drifting valve was disconnected when the regulator was opened. On no. 921 the valve was mounted on the right-hand side of the smokebox. Indicator trials were undertaken, during the course of two separate periods of tests, but no permanent alteration resulted.

In March 1941 no. 937 had left works with the standard cylinders restored and the standard Lemaitre exhaust, although retaining the extended smokebox (until October 1945) and altered balancing. Soon afterwards the fitting of multiple-jet exhausts ceased. No. 925 was in Eastleigh works in June 1941 and had· the multiple-jet exhaust fitted and was awaiting the smokebox being cut for the larger chimney when the decision was made not to proceed further with such conversions. Accordingly the modified exhaust was removed and no. 925 remained in the original condition. By this time exactly half the class had been converted (see Appendix for engines so fitted). A further and final alteration was made in the piston lead which reverted to ¼ inch for the class and in April 1942 no. 906 became its first member to be attired in the wartime black livery.

The early 1940s were not particularly happy years for the Schools because several engines became war casualties. The first of the class, no. 900, was the first to be damaged – in an incident at North Kent East Junction on 7 September 1940 – but was repaired in two weeks at Hither Green shed. Then, on

27   Severe though the damage was to no. 927, worse befell no. 934 on the night of 10/11 May 1941 on Cannon Street bridge. The engine suffered a direct hit on the cab and when dawn broke the damage was fully revealed.

D. W. Winkworth Collection

10 October of that year, no. 912 was damaged when the roof of Ewer Street depot was brought down by a bomb at 7.59 pm to be followed, on 14 October, by no. 936 plunging into a crater, which straddled nos 1 & 2 up lines just south of London Bridge, while heading the 5.10 pm Hastings–Cannon Street service. Recovery of engine and tender took until midday on 16 October and was not assisted by scares of a delayed-action bomb beneath the pierced crown of this one of the many arches which carry the railway in this area.

Next no. 927 was inside Nine Elms on the night of 16/17 April 1941 when that shed was hit by bombs and although not suffering a direct hit (as did no. 852) it had to retire to Eastleigh works for a replacement boiler, returning to traffic in July. This was quickly followed by no. 914 becoming involved in a derailment on 20 April 1941 near New Cross which required repairs so extensive as to prolong a stay at Eastleigh works until 3 January 1942. The train concerned was the 6.15 pm Charing Cross to Ramsgate (working as 6.20

pm from Cannon Street because of enemy action); at 6.31 pm between mileposts 5 and 5½ the engine, brake van and four coaches left the rails and in the process the engine hit a brick pier of bridge 108, which suffered damage for eight feet above ground level. Fireman Burgess was killed, Driver Corbin sustained head injuries but of the nine passengers injured only one was detained in hospital. The cause was the loss of a 2-inch cant of the track, following heavy rain which had undermined the track adjacent to drainage works. These had their origin in repairs to a sewer which had been burst by enemy action three weeks previously.

Worse was to come. At 4.20 am on 11 May 1941 no. 934 had a direct hit on the cab while standing on Cannon Street bridge. This was the occasion when driver Stainer of Bricklayers Arms reported '. . . the fires were like huge torches and there were thousands of sparks. The smoke from the fires blacked out the moon . . .' No. 934 was coupled to H class no. 1541 and, to save stock berthed in the fiery station, had pulled out carriages from no. 8 platform onto

65

28.   The experimental protection to the cab of no. 931 was fitted following a series of attacks by enemy aircraft, more especially in East Kent. Plans to equip twenty of the class in similar manner were never implemented.

the bridge. Bombing was so intense that the crew of no. 934 decided to abandon it each going different sides of the engine to grope his way back to the station; within seconds of their departure the locomotive was hit. After repair at Eastleigh no. 934 returned to traffic in mid-September.

Over a year elapsed before the next crop of incidents, the first of which involved no. 917 at Deal. The engine had just brought in the 3.15 pm from Charing Cross on 11 August 1942 when, at 6.15 pm, three bombs fell, as a result of which the stationmaster's house was demolished, a wall of the old engine shed was blown down and damage was inflicted on no. 917 whose driver, Cotton, received injuries which proved fatal. This same area suffered a singular series of attacks all within minutes on 31

October 1942: first bombs were dropped near Selling; then the 5.0 pm War Department recreation train from Canterbury South to Lyminge was machine-gunned near Elham (WD locomotive no. 171 was damaged); after which the luckless 3.15 pm from Charing Cross was attacked as it stood in Westenhanger station at 5.15 pm, no. 922 being disabled and driver Edwards succumbing to injuries from machine-gun fire. Finally, the 4.48 pm Ramsgate–Charing Cross train was similarly attacked at 5.20 pm when approaching Deal. No. 912 was damaged and a soldier on the train died from injuries but, fortunately, in this instance the driver, although injured, survived. Both 'Marlborough' and 'Downside' were taken to Ashford works for the cannon and machine-gun damage to be repaired and were put back into traffic very quickly by 2 November.

The railway authorities had long been concerned about the danger to footplatemen; some members of the public had been worried about trains careering out of control with the engine crew killed, while the military were interested enough to require weekly returns of attacks on trains by aircraft. This October attack seems to have brought matters to a head because in November Bulleid wrote, 'I suggest the best protection would be to cover the cab roof with plastic armour manufactured by Neuchatel Asphalte Co. . . .' He then proceeded to arrange for a locomotive to be so fitted and in due course an official inspection by railway and military officers took place. There is little doubt that the engine concerned was no. 931 which was reported at the time as having been fitted with a tender-cab, a logical step because no increase in engine weight would result and the civil engineer would not be outraged. No. 931 was then transferred to Ramsgate shed. By mid-February 1943 proposals had been drawn up to fit 200 engines in the south-east of England with

29. A victim of straffing by enemy aircraft was no. 922 'Marlborough' which was involved in one of the series of attacks made on 31 October 1942 in East Kent although damage to the engine was slight. As depicted the engine is in black livery in the last year of Southern ownership.

D. Cobbe Collection

this protection, twenty of the Schools being included, only for the whole scheme to be shelved. The very slight damage to nos 901 and 904 on 11 March 1943 at Hastings was the result of a bomb explosion rather than machine-gunning.

Meanwhile the Schools had been finding the principal trains on the Bournemouth route an increasingly arduous task owing to mounting loads and more frequent station stops. Since the summer of 1942 Nine Elms had loaned half-a-dozen Nelsons to assist and these, with their greater water capacity, were better fitted for the work now presenting itself. By January 1943 it

had been decided to shed these engines at Bournemouth on a permanent basis and so the Schools monopoly of the Bournemouth duties was broken. Nos 929, 930, 932 and 933 were transferred to Basingstoke to be joined by no. 916 from Ramsgate where no. 931 had gone with its enclosed cab arrangement. Not long after no. 929 was reported as working stopping trains between Salisbury and Exeter Central; no regular duty over this line, however, ensued.

There followed a period of relative uneventfulness with nothing other than a few reallocations to sheds to remark upon, with nos 929 and 930 getting back to Bournemouth in February 1944, to rejoin nos 924 to 928 and no. 931, after losing its tender-cab, exchanging sheds in April 1944 with no. 916 which had done duty at Basingstoke in no. 931's stead. It was about this

67

time that no. 924 worked a Royal Train from Winchester to Windsor via Staines West curve. This situation remained undisturbed until 1945 when, in April, nos 924, 925 and 926 were sent to Dover, no. 927 joining them there a little later. In the autumn of that year the metal sheets in the cab side windows began to be replaced by glass and then in January 1946 the malachite green livery supplanted the wartime black, no. 934 being the first class recipient of this cheerful shade of green to be quickly followed by nos 903, 907 and 917. In November the three Schools still remaining at Bournemouth (nos 928, 929 and 930) were moved to Brighton thus breaking the link forged in July 1937. No Schools class engine was ever to be allocated to Bournemouth again. St Leonards, on the other hand, had been gradually getting its full complement back during the year with the return at different times of nos 909 and 910.

The threads of peacetime were being taken up again and matters were returning to something approaching normality. The engines at Brighton worked the through Bournemouth, Cardiff and Plymouth services and the Hastings direct was gaining daily passengers from Tunbridge Wells and south thereof to the City. Unfortunately this return was marred by an accident involving no. 917 'Ardingly'. While heading the nine-coach 2.10 pm Victoria–Ramsgate train on 20 September 1946 at about 40 mph the engine became derailed just short of bridge no. 468 north of Catford station. For about the first hundred yards the engine and train remained coupled but then the engine broke away from the train possibly due to the left-hand running rail rising above the rear axle of the tender, piercing the vacuum reservoir and $\frac{1}{2}$-inch plate of the tender framing, going through the $\frac{3}{4}$-inch rear buffer beam of the tender and then through the cast-iron threshold plate of the leading coach threading these and the coach body before coming out of the coach a third of the way along. The engine and tender came to a halt on bridge no. 469 derailed but upright and blocking the up line while the first four coaches went down a 20-foot embankment into Catford Stadium car park. The next three coaches were derailed but stayed upright and the remaining two did not leave the track. Only one passenger was killed in the accident. The inquiry laid the blame on track irregularities stemming from maintenance arrears. 'Ardingly' returned to traffic at the end of the year after repair at Eastleigh works.

The rest of the period under company auspices brought nothing of much importance to the class. The snifting, or pressure relief, valves were made redundant on all SR engine types; the first Schools to lose the fittings was no. 918 in August 1946. The announcement on 31 October 1946 that the Southern Railway proposed to electrify or work with diesel traction all lines on the Eastern and Central Sections did pose a threat to the class, but a month later this was overshadowed by the Transport Bill with the attendant nationalisation of the railways. The threat to sweep away the Schools class from the Hastings Direct route by electric traction faded; indeed the reign was in fact to be extended for several years because of nationalisation.

6
Nationalisation

New Year's Day 1948, which heralded the start of a nationalised railway system, found the Schools class gathered on the Eastern Section at no more than four depots. Nos 900 to 910 were at St Leonards, nos 911 to 920 at Ramsgate, nos 924 to 927 at Dover with the remaining fifteen engines at Bricklayers Arms. The eleven engines at St Leonards were mainly concerned with the London traffic and probably had the most exacting tasks assigned to the class in the four up and four down business trains for which strict timekeeping was imperative. After the war commuter traffic expanded, following a popular desire to live in country areas even if working in London, so much so that the chances of a stranger getting a seat at Tunbridge Wells Central or Tonbridge on the up trains was rather slim. Even hitherto remote stations, like Etchingham, had their quota of regular City commuters and so the eleven-coach trains had all seats occupied and passengers sitting on camp stools in the corridors.

Ramsgate's duties were the Kent Coast services to London by both main routes while the Dover engines confined their work to Charing Cross or Cannon Street trains, seldom finding themselves on boat traffic to Victoria. The locomotives at Bricklayers Arms balanced the Hastings line workings of St Leonards shed by going down in the morning and returning later as well as heading certain Kent Coast services, of which the best known was the eleven-coach 9.15 am from Charing Cross. The indispensability of the class lay in the Hastings line service; other classes could adequately perform the work the Schools had been allocated elsewhere but certainly not that between Tonbridge and Hastings.

The first effects of nationalisation to become apparent were livery changes; the 'S' prefix to engine numbers was quickly followed by the 30000 addition and there were various lettering styles on the malachite green finish which still did duty for a period. Smokebox numberplates were fitted and with the bestowal of British Railways power classification 5P (the engines were the only 4–4–0s on BR to get this rating) the class was placed on a par with many 4–6–0 types of the other Regions.

As early as March 1948 no. 926 had its tender repainted at Brighton works in differing styles (one each side) of the British Railways 'sausages' type totem or logo and went up to Waterloo still in malachite green and without 'S' prefix or 30000 addition for the result to be judged by railway officers. Mercifully the rolling stock was not inflicted with the monstrosity, although it was adopted for small nameplates for stations and on printed matter. The Railway Executive decided that experimentally the most powerful express passenger engines would be painted blue, other passenger express engines green, and mixed-traffic engines in lined black. However, when these were confirmed to be the standard

30. A Schools tender in Brighton works early in the British Railways era with experimental totem painted on. Not a pretty sight!

liveries to be applied, 'other passenger express engines' was amended to read 'selected passenger', and 'mixed-traffic' engines had 'Other passenger and' placed in front. This did nothing to assuage the disappointment early in October of seeing no. 30923 turned out smartly in the black with red, cream and grey lining, because the Schools were basically express engines and deserved the green.

At about the same time that the Schools were first appearing in this new guise nos 30928 and 929 (still unrenumbered) were transferred to Stewarts Lane shed and took over the running of the Newhaven boat trains from the Atlantics. The arrangement was comparatively short-lived because no. 30929 worked the 9.5 am down and 5.55 pm up for the last time on a regular basis on 14 May 1949 to give way to the electric locomotives; subsequent appearances of the class were made on relief boat trains.

Apart from no. 30932's contretemps at Paddock Wood on 16 March, when it was derailed by going through the trap points while hauling the 4.50 am from London Bridge, the year 1949 saw the class acquiring the lined black livery and, with the collapse in Bo-Peep Tunnel in November, the breaking of new ground in regularly working to Bexhill West with the diverted Hastings trains. As an indication of the consistent work done by the Schools, it may be said that St Leonards in 1949 was heading the express passenger shed list of the Southern Region for best timekeeping records with figures such as 2.01 minutes lost per 1,000 miles run. Considering the nature of the traffic and the route involved it indicated a high level of performance by engines, enginemen and shed maintenance staff.

Half-a-dozen of the class found themselves in store for the first few months of 1950 but otherwise the routine went on completely undisturbed by any innovations of the new regime until the late fifties. The whole class had become regaled in the lined black livery when the last remaining malachite green example, no. 30917, emerged in the standard finish from Eastleigh works in July 1952.

After a gap of five years the Royal Train to

31 No. 30924 'Haileybury' leaves Sandling Junction on duty 434 on 2 September 1949. By this time the snifting valves had been removed and, although the engine had been renumbered, the tender still retained the company name.

Tattenham Corner on Derby Day was resumed in 1953. Whereas it had last been worked by light Pacifics, from 1953 until withdrawal of the class, it became the undisputed preserve of the Schools. No. 30915 officiated in 1953, no. 30936 the next year, followed by no. 30933 in 1955. In 1956 the State visit to Sweden rendered the train unnecessary. On its return in 1957 no. 30939 was in charge, the honour in 1958 falling to no. 30908, in 1959 to no. 30938 and in 1960 to no. 30925. The last two occasions when a Schools worked the train (1961 and 1962) the representative was no. 30926 'Repton', the sole locomotive to take the duty more than once. Another royal occasion for which a Schools was used was for the Review of the Royal Air Force by the Queen at Odiham on 15 July 1953, when no. 30937 hauled the train from Waterloo to Winchfield and back to London from Hook.

Typical of the demands made upon the class in the first decade of BR is the summer of 1954.

At the beginning of the summer timetable the forty locomotives were distributed over five depots, one of which had but one engine and no booked duty for it. Each weekday there were twenty duties for the class, rising to no less than thirty-seven on Saturdays for, in effect, thirty-nine engines and falling to fifteen on Sundays. Obviously there was spare capacity for the Monday–Friday turns and on those days washing-out and repairs could be carried out without jeopardising the availability of the class. It was on Saturdays that the requirement was at its maximum and so it was desirable that visits to works be avoided between June and September.

Nos 30900 to 30910 were, as customary, shedded at St Leonards. These eleven engines had eight weekday duties allocated with one more on Saturdays. Duty 395 consisted of working the five-coach 6.22 am ex Hastings local service to Tonbridge, standing there as

32. The collapse in Bo-Peep Tunnel towards the end of 1949 brought the class regularly onto the Bexhill West branch. The distinctive roof of the station will be noted in this picture of no. 30903 'Charterhouse' leaving on an up relief train on Easter Monday 1957, some years after the trouble with the tunnel.

S. C. Nash

emergency during the morning and then taking the 1.57 pm to Charing Cross and heading the 5.29 pm back to Hastings. The six coach 6.58 am from Hastings was the start of duty 396; after calling locally to Crowhurst the next stops were Tunbridge Wells, Tonbridge (where the five coaches of the 6.22 am from Hastings were attached), Hildenborough and Sevenoaks with an arrival at Cannon Street at 8.47 am. The engine next worked the 10.25 am from Charing Cross to Hastings and the 2.10 pm return before tackling the eleven-coach 6.3 pm departure from Cannon Street, a heavy and fast business service calling at Tunbridge Wells Central, Wadhurst and all stations from Battle to Hastings.

Duty 397 encompassed two most important business trains: the up service 7.27 am from Hastings which served stations to Crowhurst, then Etchingham and Tunbridge Wells Central whence it was fast to Cannon Street with an arrival at 9.9 am; the evening return eleven-coach 5.6 pm from Cannon Street with a 47½ minute non-stop timing to Tunbridge Wells after which calls balancing the 7.27 am up were made. Between these prestigious trains the

engine worked, tender first, the little-publicised 9.27 am Cannon Street–Charing Cross passenger service (the continuation of the 7.27 am Ashford–Cannon Street train).

Next in the list, duty 398 involved up and down business trains of a slower nature in the 7.40 am up Cannon Street service and the 5.18 pm return. Last of the morning business trains was the 8.10 am which, between Crowhurst and Cannon Street, called at Wadhurst and Tunbridge Wells. Forming part of 399 duty, it was followed by the 2.25 pm Charing Cross–Hastings, the 6.54 pm Hastings–Ashford and 8.53 pm return to Hastings which finished a long day's work. The fast late morning up Hastings service (11.10 am departure) calling at Tunbridge Wells and Sevenoaks formed the first part of duty 400 with the 4.20 pm ex Charing Cross semi-fast back completing the task.

The 7.22 am Hastings–Ashford, 9.30 am Ashford–Tonbridge and 11.28 am Tonbridge–Hastings stopping trains formed the first leg of duty 401, followed by a return trip to London on the 3.20 pm from Hastings and 7.25 pm out of Charing Cross. The next duty (402) was a rather sedate, although prolonged, affair which

72

33. Detail from one of the five windows in Wellington College chapel which were dedicated on 2 November 1952. Designed by Hugh Easton on the theme of *Benedicite Omnia Opera*, to replace windows shattered by enemy action in October 1940, the fifth window includes no. 902 on an eleven-coach train.

Mike Esau. By kind permission of Wellington College

started with the 6.20 am to Ashford and 9.12 am return, continued with the 1.10 pm all stations to Tonbridge, 3.22 pm thence to Cannon Street and ended with the 6.22 pm from Charing Cross.

On Saturdays there were variations on these rosters because of the absence of evening business traffic. Two Saturday-only diagrams for the shed took Schools along the coast over the Central Section to Brighton. Duty 403 included getting the empty stock for the 8.48 am Hastings–Wolverhampton service down from Crowhurst, then working the train to Brighton, picking up the corresponding down train and working it to Eastbourne, turning and taking the 10.40 am Birmingham–Hastings train to its destination and rounding off the day with a return trip to Ashford. The other Saturday-only trip (407) was similar to 403 without the Ashford trip. On Sunday there was a day of rest – but not for the shed staff! There was only one duty (395) to be coped with which covered two return trips, the first to Ashford and the other to Charing Cross. So ten of St Leonards' eleven Schools would be available for attention on a Sunday, special traffic requirements permitting.

Ramsgate's allocation of eight engines (nos 30911 to 30914, 30916 to 30918 and 30922) had three weekday duties – 477, 478 and 481. The first of these was made up of the 7.3 am Margate–Cannon Street via Canterbury West with the 6.18 pm return to Ramsgate via Dover (on Saturdays the 4.34 pm from Charing Cross); the second involved the 8.20 am Herne Bay–Cannon Street and for the return varied according to date with either the 6.15 pm or 7.34 pm or (for Saturdays) the 2.20 pm departures from London; the third turn was the straightforward 1.55 pm Ramsgate–Victoria and 8.35 pm return. On Saturdays there were five extra duties (479, 480, 483, 484 and 492) all of which, except for the last, were basically one return trip from Thanet to London. The exception was the 8.55 am Margate to Redhill and the 12.8 pm return. Sundays saw all Ramsgate's Schools confined to shed.

Stewarts Lane had no. 30915 'Brighton' allocated, but no regular duty although primarily it was for use on relief Newhaven boat workings. With summer demands of the Channel port traffic particularly heavy, Stewarts Lane could – and did – put the locomotive to good use, for on

73

34. The large BR lion emblem and the lining carried up to the top edge of the tender is sported by no. 30930 'Radley' in May 1953, seen climbing Hildenborough bank with a Kent Coast relief train.

Brian Morrison

the very first Saturday of that summer's time-table it was noted working duty 33, officially a job for a six-wheel tender King Arthur from Victoria to Margate.

Engines nos 30919 to 30921 and 30923 were stationed at Dover which had two weekday and Sunday duties and four on Saturdays. It therefore shared with Ramsgate the necessity of a 100 per cent turn-out of its allocation on summer Saturdays. Duty 433 included the 8.59 am Dover Priory to Charing Cross, empty stock working as far out as Grove Park and the 7.34 pm return to Folkestone Junction (varied during high summer to 6.16 pm ex Cannon Street to Ramsgate via Faversham and 11.0 pm Ramsgate–Dover Priory). Duty 434 covered the 11.6 am Dover Priory–Charing Cross and return 4.15 pm 'Man of Kent' to Margate with the 9.28 pm Margate–Dover Priory mail train to finish the day. On Saturdays duty 433 was altered to cover the 1.57 pm Charing Cross–Deal via Maidstone East and duty 434 extended

to Ashford with the mail train returning with the 2.18 am mail to Dover Priory and the 3.30 am van train to Dover Marine. The extra Saturday duties – 426 and 436 – involved, in the first instance a round trip to Victoria via Deal and Faversham and, in the other case, the 9.40 am Deal–Charing Cross via Maidstone East and 3.5 pm return to Deal. Sunday duty 433 was made up of the 6.55 am Dover Priory–Charing Cross, 7.0 pm Charing Cross–Ashford and 11.31 pm Ashford–Deal mail. Also on Sundays duty 434 incorporated the 10.20 am Dover Marine up van train and the 9.15 pm passenger Charing Cross to Dover Priory.

The remaining sixteen Schools (nos 30924 to 30939) resided at Bricklayers Arms which had a rather odd requirement for the class with seven weekday duties, fifteen Saturday rosters and no less than twelve Sunday workings. The first duty – 80 – consisted of a double trip to Hastings. Duty 81 gave the keen observer an opportunity to note a Schools on a coal train –

35. In 1955 the Victoria–Tattenham Corner Royal Derby special was entrusted to no. 30933 'King's-Canterbury'. The splendid condition of the engine with white cab roof was well captured by the camera in the vicinity of Chipstead.

D. W. Winkworth Collection

the 3.20 am Bricklayers Arms Goods to Cannon Street – after which followed a jaunt over the Central Section with the 4.50 am London Bridge – Redhill – Ashford – Margate service. Next came the 11.23 am Ramsgate to Margate, the 12.36 pm Margate–Charing Cross, 6.23 pm Cannon Street–Faversham–Dover Priory and the busy day was nicely rounded off by working the 10.30 pm mail train from Dover Priory to Cannon Street via Redhill. Duty 82 was mainly a Hastings line turn starting with the 5.45 am London Bridge–Hastings, 10.10 am Hastings–Charing Cross and continuing with the 3.25 pm Charing Cross–Wadhurst returning tender first at 4.56 pm to Tonbridge, where the engine stood as evening emergency engine for down traffic before taking the 8.58 pm train up to Charing Cross.

The star working for the shed was contained in duty 83 which had the 9.15 am Charing Cross–Ramsgate and the 2.45 pm Margate–Dover–Redhill–Cannon Street return as its revenue-earning trains. Duty 84 was a Hastings 'rounder': 9.25 am ex Charing Cross, 1.28 pm ex Hastings and 4.10 pm ex Ashford to Charing Cross. Duty 86 had a simple return trip to Ashford with van and empty stock workings

finishing activities for the turn at Rotherhithe Road at 2.52 am. The 8.25 am Charing Cross–Hastings started duty 87, which had a round trip Hastings–Ashford before returning to London with the 7.10 pm from Hastings.

Most of the foregoing Bricklayers Arms duties operated on Saturdays with amendments. For example duty 82 dropped the 10.10 am Hastings–Charing Cross and the Wadhurst working in favour of a return Hastings–Ashford passenger train followed by an engine-and-brake trip from St Leonards West Marina to Galley Hill and the return freight which had a journey of three minutes duration! The 2.56 pm passenger from Hastings got the engine back to Tonbridge to resume with the 8.58 pm train to Charing Cross. The Saturday-only duties naturally covered return trips to Hastings (duties 85 and 88) although the majority were Deal 'rounders'. Saturdays also saw some longer empty stock stabling trips to exotic sub-urban outposts like Bellingham, Orpington and Blackheath; one of these duties (95) even worked in a freight train from Plumstead to Bricklayers Arms!

Sundays were by no means rest days for Bricklayers Arms engines. There were five

36. Nine Elms duty 22 being worked by no. 30912 'Downside' at Sherborne. The shield over the AWS gear at the front of the engine and the piping thereto along the framing is noticeable.

W. Philip Conolly

duties (80, 81, 82, 83 and 87) for return Ramsgate/Margate trains, three (84, 85 and 86) Hastings returns (of which the middle one incorporated an extra up journey having stabled overnight at St Leonards for the purpose), one Hastings/Ashford 'rounder' (duty 90) and the pleasure-seekers' excursions (duty 94 to Deal, 98 to Hastings and 100 up from Deal after overnight stabling at Ramsgate).

Dominance of the scene by the Schools at both St Leonards and Bricklayers Arms depots is well illustrated by the mileages run individually, collectively and comparatively by those members gathered at the latter shed, in this case for the week ending 14 July 1951 when the work was little different from that just described. For this summer week the total mileage run by the shed's eighty-two engines was 41,892 of which no less than 14,835 was by seventeen Schools. At this time Bricklayers

Arms had three King Arthurs and eighteen Schools (nos 30922 to 30939) as its front-rank passenger power, the Schools being neatly divided equally between single and multiple blastpipe examples. No. 30922 was stopped awaiting works and did not turn a wheel during the week but otherwise all engines did some work ranging from 143 miles by no. 30935 to 1,515 by no. 30933. Seven of the class ran four-figure mileages, these being nos 30924 (1,032), 30925 (1,329), 30927 (1,346), 30928 (1,384), 30929 (1,200), 30933 (1,515) and 30937 (1,141). The average per engine for the seventeen working was 873 miles. Only 2–6–4 tanks nos 42081 and 42082 of the shed's other engines reached four-figure mileages (1,319 and 1,123 respectively) during the week. In complete contrast, the couple of old LBSCR Atlantics (nos 32037 and 32038) were not called upon to cover more than 87 miles each in their dotage!

7
Latter Days

Seven years elapsed before British Railways announced a modernisation scheme. Then it transpired that, so far as the Southern Region was concerned, it was 1947 all over again with electrification proposed for the main lines in Kent, which meant that the Schools had enjoyed a reprieve of about eight years. Thought had already been given to the replacement of the carriage stock on the Hastings direct service and a decision had been made on such a programme. Modernisation, however, offered the opportunity to make the new stock electric multiple-unit sets; the disadvantage with that was that the stock would be ready before trackwork could be completed. After some indecision, as well as pressure from commuter groups, it was stated in the autumn of 1955 that diesel-electric traction in the form of multiple-units would be introduced on a small scale by the summer of 1957 to be followed later by a complete coverage of traffic by that type of motive power, making a 90-minute journey between London and Hastings possible. So the writing was on the wall for the Schools and so it was the more curious that the class shortly began to regain the green livery it had been denied for several years.

The new stock started to be turned out from Eastleigh works in January 1957 and began trial running so that by February training trips on the Hastings line were in progress. The first ten sets were short-frame formations, each coach being 56 ft 11 in. long, which points to the adaptation

of the frames of the proposed replacement steam stock; later sets had frames 6 ft 6 in. longer.

Destruction of the signal-box at Cannon Street by fire altered the intention to put the new traction to work with the start of the summer timetable in June. It was decided to introduce the new stock on the service on 6 May 1957 when the temporary signal-box was commissioned, as this would cut down on light engine movements and so assist the signalmen in their task.

Stage I of the new service was inaugurated on 17 June and as a result the allocation of Schools class engines at St Leonards shed was reduced to just three engines, nos 30900 to 30902. The others were transferred away in the main to Nine Elms where an immediate appearance on the Lymington Pier Saturday trains as well as Bournemouth services followed. For the start of the winter timetable restrictions on the class going to Yeovil Town were lifted and the first regular duty (Nine Elms 22) for a Schools west of Salisbury was introduced, even though it was nothing more than a local service.

Rebuilding of the light Pacifics was also proceeding apace with the Eastern Section being the principal beneficiary. This meant that for the first time in the history of the Schools their pattern of duties was becoming diffused, so that members of the class were much more frequently powering special turns – for example, Southampton Docks and relief Newhaven boat

37. No. 30919 'Harrow' leaves Groombridge on a stopping train from Tunbridge Wells West to Brighton on 14 May 1960, a typical latter day duty for the class.

D. W. Winkworth

trains – and making trips to places, such as Swale Halt, which had never seen a Schools before.

The final break with St Leonards shed came with the implementation of Stage II of the Hastings diesel scheme on 9 June 1958. Nos 30900 to 30902 were transferred away and the tradition of almost twenty-seven years was at an end, although no one locomotive had spent the whole of the period there. The nearest approach to that was by no. 30904 which had an unbroken run until June 1957. Certainly no other Schools engine approached this record for this or any other shed.

Reliance on the class in Kent on summer Saturdays was still heavy, even in 1958, as witness a six-hour period of observation in the Whitstable/Herne Bay area on 26 July. Of the sixty-four trains noted no less than fifteen were Schools-hauled which included thirteen individual locomotives two of which, such as

no. 30916 on duty 485 (up and down 'Kentish Belle'), were seen twice. Thus the class provided over 20 per cent of the motive power.

Extension of the range of the class was made in October 1958 when Oxted line duties were undertaken and in the next month came the report of a working between Redhill and Reading. On 19 December no. 30939 headed a special from Horsham via Three Bridges to Kensington, and on Christmas Eve no. 30925 made a welcome return to the Hastings direct line with the 3.58 pm ex Charing Cross relief train. In 1959 the class went even further afield with no. 30906 at Alton with a football excursion on 24 January and the introduction of a duty between Brighton and Tonbridge. Improvements and additional equipment at this late stage were made to the class: automatic warning system gear as well as blowdown valve gear and water treatment started to be fitted in April 1959; briquette carriers first appeared in

38.   Detail of speedometer and that part of the AWS gear placed just forward of the cab.

John F. W. Paige

August; manganese steel liners to coupled wheels in October and speedometers in November.

With the completion of Stage I of the Kent electrification scheme there had to be a general reshuffle of the class, and from mid-June 1959 the allocation became:

Brighton: nos 30900, 30901, 30914 and 30915
Nine Elms: nos 30902/3/6/7/9, 30910 to 30913, 30916 to 30919
Basingstoke: nos 30904, 30905 and 30908
Stewarts Lane: nos 30920 to 30923
Bricklayers Arms: nos 30924 to 30931
Ashford: nos 30932 to 30937
Dover: nos 30938 and 30939

Nine Elms had acted as a dumping ground for locomotives displaced by the Kent electrification and so it was not surprising that nos 30916 and 30917 were transferred away within a month to Brighton and nos 30903, 30906 and 30909 followed, in March 1960, to Guildford to take over Redhill–Reading line duties. Nos 30914, 30915 and 30916 moved to Redhill the next month to assist on similar turns as well as to

power the 5.25 pm London Bridge–Reading train and the 7.27 am up balancing working. As further variety for the class, from mid-August Stewarts Lane used its allocation on the Glasgow–Eastbourne car sleeper trains.

Ashford works' involvement in repairing the class had increased very markedly over the five years from 1955 and it was from there that the first withdrawals of the class were made, in January 1961, involving nos 30919 and 30932. Both locomotives still carried BR lined black livery; no. 30919 was cut up during the week ending 11 March but its companion lingered on the scrap road for several months being joined during this time by no. 30933 which was awaiting its fate – either to be scrapped or preserved in Canterbury. Withdrawals became regular, although not in large numbers, and so it was strange that two of the class got coupled to Lord Nelson eight-wheeled tenders, no. 30912 in June and no. 30921 in November 1961. It was stated that this change was made to assist the class in working freight trains because the larger tender would provide additional braking power. That the acquisition of these tenders did not proceed beyond these two is not very

79

Mike Esau

39.   A late summer scene with no. 30917 'Ardingly' powering a twelve-coach inter-regional train along the Tonbridge—Redhill route.

40.   In 1960 efforts were made to improve the riding characteristics of the Kent Coast electric multiple-unit buffet cars. Car S69008 was marshalled in a BR standard four-coach set, piped through for vacuum, and, with different swing link configurations, underwent a series of tests. On 20 April 1960 no. 30920 'Rugby' is pictured before leaving Lancing works and reaching a maximum of 83 mph en route to London Bridge, successfully unseating observers in the buffet car in the process!

C. P. Boocock

41. The 9.42 am Waterloo–Lymington Pier service in charge of no. 30910 'Merchant Taylors' approaches Southampton Central on 6 August 1960. The road traffic sign 'Crossing No Gates' is a reminder of the connection which had existed for many years from the siding near the tunnel to the electricity works.

surprising because the Schools were not really suited to freight services, there were enough freight engines still available, the supply of Lord Nelson tenders was limited in any case to fifteen and, by no means least of all, the days of the Schools were already numbered.

Whereas before nationalisation there is no record of engines changing tenders with others of the class it was not unusual in BR days. The tender numbers ran from 700 to 739 and were paired in strict sequence with the engines nos 900 to 939. Those tenders which found second, or third, attachments were: 703 – no. 30906 (April 1962); 705 – no. 30932 (August 1958); 706 – no. 30903 (April 1962); 708 – no. 30901 (September 1949), no. 30908 (October 1949); 710 – no. 30928 (May 1955), no. 30921 (August 1957); 711 – no. 30939 (March 1955); 713 – no. 30936 (April 1954), no. 30933 (October 1957); 714 – no. 30928 (August 1957); 720 – no. 30914 (September 1957); 721 – no. 30920 (September 1957); 722 – no. 30924 (November 1952); 723 – no. 933 (March 1948), no. 30936 (November 1957); 724 – no. 30922 (November 1952); 728 – no. 30910 (April 1955); 731 – no. 30916 (February 1962); 732 – no. 30905 (August 1958); 733 – no. 923 (March 1948); 736 – no. 30913 (May 1954); 738 – no. 30937 (September 1961) and 739 – no. 30911 (March 1955).

Tender 732 got repainted in BR green livery in Ashford works in error and because no. 30932 remained in lined black livery it had to have a black-liveried tender and so a straight exchange was done with no. 30905, which was black but was going into the green livery. So no. 30905

D. W. Winkworth

42.   No. 30921 'Shrewsbury' calls at Sandhurst Halt on 27 October 1962 with the 12.5 pm ex Reading (Southern) local service. The Lord Nelson type tender (1007) had been acquired a year previously.

43.   One of the freight duties for which the Lord Nelson tenders might have proved useful was the Brighton—Eastbourne freight. Here no. 30907 'Dulwich' approaches Polegate on that duty on 19 February 1961.

S. C. Nash

44.   High-sided tender 732 was transferred from no. 30932 to no. 30905 'Tonbridge' in August 1958. This view illustrates the final method of lining-out the cab side with the lining terminating at the running plate in the bottom leading side.

got the sole high-sided tender of the class for its last few years. It is not without interest that of the five tenders (705 to 709) which had already done duty with King Arthur or Lord Nelson engines before being attached to the Schools, three had changes, and to complete a varied career 708 was transferred to S15 class 4–6–0 no. 30833 in May 1962. A month later 712 was also coupled to an S15 class engine – no. 30837.

By 1 January 1962 there had been fifteen withdrawals, and other engines had been incarcerated at the back of sheds in unserviceable con-

dition. The first of the class, 'Eton', had thus languished at Brighton for about a year before withdrawal during January to be cut up at Ashford in mid-March. Eighteen years later its file in the Public Record Office still indicated that it had been preserved! Final mileage figures for individual members of the class were around the one million mark. As an example no. 30938 went into traffic on 19 July 1935 with boiler 1038 and tender 738 (which it retained until withdrawal), and had nine general overhauls and twenty-three other visits to works of which one was merely for photographic purposes. The mileages between the general repairs were (figures in brackets are intermediate mileages at

45.   The Schools did not often stray onto foreign metals. However no. 30925 did find itself piloting another 4—4—0 type (no. 40646) on a railtour special at York on 13 May 1962. On its way home it was used in ordinary traffic on the old Great Central section working on at least four occasions the 6.10 pm Marylebone—Woodford, then light engine to Banbury and a milk train back to Marylebone.

boiler changes and are not to be counted in the total):

Date	Boiler	Mileage	
May 1937	1013	79,378	
May 1938	1021	(43,427)	
February 1939	1009	81,535	
June 1940	1040	(55,058)	
September 1941	1012	93,987	Eastleigh works
January 1944	1022	97,180	
March 1946	1035	87,274	
March 1949	1024	110,883	
September 1953	1011	188,531	
October 1956	1036	94,178	
December 1958	1029	66,248	Ashford works
March 1960	—	(34,442)	
8 July 1961	Withdrawn	say 65,000	

The total mileage was in the region of 965,000 for an engine built last but one and with an early withdrawal date. Scheduled mileage for a general repair in BR days was 85,000 and so no. 30938 had a good average against this figure. The September 1953 mileage was by no means a freak figure as many of the class returned such good results among the best being 213,903 and 205,487 (both by no. 30917) and 222,687 by no. 30912. Certainly from the maintenance standpoint the class had few shortcomings.

The survivors carried on manfully during 1962 and would still turn up with regularity on a Nine Elms duty which had been evolved a few years previously to get a Schools down as far as Exeter Central. No. 30926 worked the

46. No. 30938 'St Olave's' enters Dover Priory on 24 September 1955. Another year was to elapse before it would enter Ashford works after running 94,178 miles since its previous general overhaul in September 1953.

customary Derby Day Royal Train but by the beginning of December the ranks of the class had thinned to seventeen and as one saw some of those operating early that month without name-plates it was realised the end could not be far away; indeed it transpired that accountancy purposes demanded the complete withdrawal of the class by 29 December 1962. No. 30911 worked the 4.40 pm London Bridge to Brighton on 28 December, the last passenger service movement by a Schools on the Central Section, and next day was dumped along with nos 30901, 30915 and 30923 at Hove. The last member of the class to be in steam was no. 30934 which took a 700 class 0–6–0 and itself from Basing-stoke to Eastleigh on 18 May 1963.

So the Schools completed their career sud-denly, yet it had been on borrowed time for, if the Southern Railway had electrified to Hastings after the war as intended, redundancy would have come sooner. Of the forty engines, three were sold for scrapping in Northampton-shire, fourteen were broken up at Ashford, twenty were cut up at Eastleigh and three, all from the contingent once shedded at Bourne-mouth, very happily have survived to keep green the memory of the golden years of the class.

85

8
Post-War Performance

After the war the Schools were to be seen comparatively little on the Western Section until ousted from their Kentish haunts, and by then the duties left were mainly of a secondary nature. Railtour trains, such as no. 30929 running from Portsmouth Harbour to Waterloo in 89 minutes 21 seconds (86 minutes net) with six bogies, did not often extend the engines while the Saturday-only Lymington Pier trains seldom yielded much in the way of performance data, probably because of the congested state of the line on summer Saturdays and the lower-link crews not being accustomed to handling the class. One of the better efforts, recorded by Mr A. G. S. Davies on 29 August 1959, was of no. 30911 with ten coaches (324/330 tons) on the 12 noon from Waterloo. Checked even before reaching Vauxhall and with a relaying restriction at Woking, milepost 31 was passed in 39½ minutes at 57 mph; from there on to Worting Junction (passed in 58½ minutes) the maximum speed was 65 mph and after getting up to 77 mph at Weston signal box no. 30911 was eased. A dead stand outside Southampton Central made the elapsed time to that station 91¾ minutes but the net time was no more than 82¼ minutes, not greatly removed from pre-war practice although with a lighter loading. In the up direction Mr B. I. Nathan caught no. 30913 working the eleven-vehicle (380/415 tons) 11.25 am boat train from Southampton New Docks on 19 September 1959 when a steady climb was made from Eastleigh to Roundwood (23¼ minutes for the 17.3 miles), speed varying only between 43 and 50 mph on the climb. Maximum speeds inwards to London were 68 mph west of Woking and 72 mph east thereof.

Some of the Nine Elms contingent, as well as Guildford members, found work on the Reading–Redhill line. With a four-coach local train there was obviously no problem, but with a twelve-coach assignment it was a different matter, especially between Guildford and Redhill. Eastward there is the six-mile climb through Chilworth and Gomshall culminating in nearly two miles at 1 in 96 to milepost 33¾. After the Deepdene dip comes a further climb to Betchworth finishing at 1 in 118 before the final ascent into Reigate at 1 in 142. In table 14 detail A no. 30924 kept good time on the westbound run to Dorking Town and surmounted the summit of the 1 in 96 before Gomshall at 30 mph to get the Birkenhead train into Guildford over two minutes early. Eastbound no. 30930 with twelve coaches had the advantage over no. 30924 with its thirteen vehicles and this is reflected in the running. This was a frustrating train to record as invariably any gain would be rewarded by signal stops at the conclusion of the journey; even so it was still a fascinating exercise in the study of performance.

The Central Section had various duties from time to time for the class such as the Brighton–

Table 14. REDHILL – GUILDFORD

	A	Detail	B	C
Date	28 Oct. 1961	Date	1 Sep. 1962	12 Aug. 1961
Locomotive no.	30924 (L)	Locomotive no.	30930 (L)	30924 (L)
Vehicles	12	Vehicles	12	13
Tare load (tons)	382	Tare load (tons)	396	434
Gross load (tons)	400	Gross load (tons)	425	455
Recorder	A. G. S. Davies	Recorder	Author	A. G. S. Davies

Mls	Sch.	m. s.	Spd		Mls	Sch.	m. s.	Spd	m. s.	Spd
0.0	0	0 00		REDHILL	20.4	38	40 00		38 46	
							sig. stop		sig. stop	
1.8		4 53	33/56	Reigate	18.6		33 25		29 27	
							sig. stop			
4.7		8 25	50	Betchworth	15.7		24 10	45	25 38	55
7.3		11 08	61	Deepdene	13.2		21 16	66	22 48	60/48
8.0	12	11 54	40/30	DORKING TOWN	12.4	23	20 35	66	22 10	64
12.8		19 02	60	Gomshall	7.7		14 30	46/30	15 56	45/32
16.7		23 01	68	Chilworth	3.8		7 25	35/26	7 52	28/26
18.5		24 45	71	Shalford	1.9		4 38	38	4 34	36
19.2	29	26 41		*Shalford Jc.*★	1.2	3	3 32	30	3 24	
20.4	32	29 48		GUILDFORD	0.0	0	0 00		0 00	
		29¾		Estimated net time (mins)			32		33½	

★Speed restriction

Bournemouth or Salisbury duties and the Newhaven boat trains. Timekeeping runs seem to have been the order of the day with the boat trains and little more. A return trip made behind no. 30929 in May 1949 hauling thirteen vehicles from Victoria to Newhaven produced no higher speed than 60 mph on the return, although 69 mph had been the maximum going down. Two runs between Polegate and Brighton with the 12.56 pm Birmingham (Snow Hill) service timed by Mr R. A. H. Weight, each loaded to eleven coaches (about 370 tons full), had nos 30900 and 30909 pass Kemp Town Junction in 26 minutes 40 seconds and 27 minutes 6 seconds respectively (schedule 27½ minutes) only to be blocked outside Brighton and arrive a minute late on each occasion. The best speed was 69 mph by no. 30900 at Glynde, net time for the 19.8 miles, which included over three miles climb at 1 in 88 after the 10 mph restriction at Lewes, being in the region of 30 minutes.

Undoubtedly it was the Eastern Section that saw the best running in post-war years. The fitting of the Lemaitre exhaust to half the class came too late to make any impression on pre-war performance, but after the conflict many of the best runs with Schools were with those having the modified exhaust. Some prolonged discussion on the topic was conducted in the columns of the *Railway Magazine* in support of the superiority of the modified engines. Officially there was never any difference in

Stanley Creer

47. No. 30911 'Dover' heads an Eastbourne–Walsall train northwards on the Quarry line near Merstham.

48. No. 30918 'Hurstpierpoint' passing North Pole Junction with the 11.5 am Margate–Kidsgrove inter-regional train on 8 August 1959.

R. C. Riley

Table 15. WATERLOO – FOLKESTONE CENTRAL

	A		Detail	B		C
Date	29 Aug. 1955		Date	16 May 1957		30 June 1955
Train	4.17 pm		Train	5.11 pm		2.36 pm
Loco. no.	30919 (L)		Loco. no.	30935		30925
Vehicles	11		Vehicles	10		11
Tare	370		Tare load (tons)	329		368
Gross	395		Gross load (tons)	350		385
Recorder	K. J. Baker		Recorder	A. J. Baker		K. J. Baker

Mls	Sch.	m. s.	Speed		Mls	Sch.	m. s.	Speed	Sch.	m. s.	Speed
0.0	0	0 00		WATERLOO	55.3	65	65 06		66	67 42	
1.1	3	2 57		LONDON BRIDGE★	54.3	62½	62 28		63	65 01	
							sigs	30		sigs	10
4.1	7	6 49	58	New Cross	51.3		57 43	49	58	58 35	47
							sigs	32		sigs	28
6.4	10	9 29	50	Hither Green	48.9	55	54 14	56	55	55 12	71
							sigs	40			
8.3		11 44	46	Grove Park	47.2		51 53	66		53 34	64
10.5	15½	14 40	51	Chislehurst	44.9	51½	49 41	62	51	51 20	
										pws	18
13.0	18½	17 36	60	ORPINGTON	42.3	49	47 12	67	48	46 47	73
15.8		20 37	51	Knockholt	39.6		44 22	43		43 53	43
19.8		24 23	74	Dunton Green	35.6		39 45	65		39 03	65
21.3	28	25 51	60/58	SEVENOAKS T.H.	34.0	39	38 02	33	39	37 24	37
							sigs	18			
26.2		30 15	82	Hildenborough	29.1		28 30	52		29 46	
28.8	35½	32 40	45	TONBRIDGE★	26.6	27	25 32	51	27	26 39	51
34.1	41	38 07	73	Paddock Wood	21.3	22	20 27	82	22	21 35	74
38.6		42 02	65	Marden	16.7		17 11	71		17 43	66
41.1		44 14	77	Staplehurst	14.2		15 06			15 32	
		pws	47								
44.5		47 20	57	Headcorn	10.9		12 27	80		12 46	77
49.7		53 11	66/61	Pluckley	5.7		8 08	68		8 20	68
55.3	60½	58 36	68	ASHFORD	0.0	0	0 00		0	0 00	
59.6		62 55	57/61	Smeeth							
63.4		66 49	58	Westenhanger							
64.7		68 10	64	Sandling Junc.							
68.5		72 24		Shorncliffe							
69.2	76½	73 45		FOLKESTONE CEN.							
		72		Estimated net time (mins)			60¾			63½	

★Speed restriction

89

the duties allocated, the only note ever being appended in the Engine Workings book was that Schools class engines on the Kent 'rounders' were to be fully coaled. The Lemaitre-equipped engines could demonstrate an advantage due to the decrease in back-pressure the fitting afforded, but an allied factor was the tendency of drivers to handle these engines rather more energetically due to driving by ear on the thin rasping exhaust. This is borne out by records of heavier coal consumption (about 1 lb. per mile more) for the modified examples of the class, which for equal work performed would be expected to show a saving of a few pounds per mile.

A good demonstration of the prowess of the modified engines comes in table 15 detail A which may be compared with runs in table 1 (incidentally the Lemaitre-fitted engines are indicated in the tables by 'L' in parenthesis); this run on the 'Man of Kent' needs no further comment as to its excellence and the two up runs from Ashford indicate that the original design could produce some swift running when necessary. It was the 9.15 am from Charing Cross that gave the class a chance to show what could be done between Tonbridge and Ashford, and table 16 (all runs from Mr A. J. Baker's records) sets out the best run that can be traced with each class variety, and this is extended to the up 4.55 pm which tended to include four-wheeled vans with their greater drag. It must be stressed that these were not light four-coach formations, and the work performed was of the highest quality.

Probably the finest climb of Sole Street bank

Table 16. TONBRIDGE – ASHFORD

A	B	Detail	C	D
23 July 1953	23 Dec. 1954	Date	14 May 1953	13 July 1950
10.4 am	10.4 am	Train	4.55 pm	4.55 pm
30926	30931 (L)	Locomotive no.	30926	30919 (L)
11	11	Vehicles	9	12
363	365	Tare load (tons)	247	292
400	390	Gross load (tons)	265	310
Todd (BA)	Jakes (BA)	Driver	Mills (AFD)	Morman (AFD)

Mls	Sch.	m. s.	Spd	m. s.	Spd		Mls	Sch.	m. s.	Spd	m. s.	Spd
0.0	0	0 00		0 00		TONBRIDGE	26.6	32	29 12		26 31	
											pws	25
5.4	8	7 46	71/76	7 39	72	Paddock Wood	21.3	25	22 30	61	20 26	78
									pws	35		
9.9		11 29	69	11 14	81	Marden	16.7		16 49	68/71	16 55	72
12.4		13 29		13 11	75	Staplehurst	14.2		14 42	78	14 57	
15.7		16 02	81	15 41	84/76	Headcorn	10.9		12 07	82	12 26	82
20.9		20 14	71/76	19 43	84	Pluckley	5.7		7 55	71/68	8 16	71/69
24.4		23 13	70/74	22 26	77/81	Chart Siding	2.2		4 19	48	4 40	46
26.6	31	25 46		25 18		ASHFORD	0.0	0	0 00		0 00	
		25¾		25¼		Estimated net time (mins)			26¾		26	

ever made by a Schools was recorded by Mr A. J. Baker on 12 June 1959 when no. 30938 (modified engine) hauling ten coaches (332/350 tons), with driver Deacon of Stewarts Lane in charge, passed Farningham Road at 83 mph in 17 minutes 12 seconds from the Chatham start before permanent way checks curbed the effort. Cuxton Road signal-box was passed in 5 minutes 56 seconds at 48 mph, Sole Street in 11 minutes 29 seconds (41 mph), Fawkham in exactly 15 minutes at 81 mph and Bromley

South was reached in 30 minutes 39 seconds (27½ minutes net).

The calibre of running, if a little less flamboyant, was no whit lower on the Hastings route, where consistency was paramount. In table 17 are four fine non-stop runs from London to Tunbridge Wells. Detail A offers what is believed to be the fastest actual (as well as net) time on record by the class. Mr S. C. Nash noted the train as being 1½ minutes late away and this presumably resulted in a clear road

Table 17. CANNON STREET – TUNBRIDGE WELLS CENTRAL

Detail		A				B				C				D		
Date		23 Sep. 1957				8 Oct. 1955				1955				—		
Train		5.5 pm				12.18 pm				6.3 pm				5.6 pm		
Locomotive no.		30914 (L)				30926				30909 (L)				30910		
Vehicles		8				10				11				11		
Tare load (tons)		268				336				348				358		
Gross load (tons)		295				360				380				380		
Mls		Sch.	m.	s.	Spd	Sch.	m.	s.	Spd	Sch.	m.	s.	Spd	m.	s.	Spd
0.0	CANNON STREET	0	0	00		0	0	00		0	0	00		0	00	
0.7	LONDON BRIDGE★	2½	1	41		2½	2	42		2½	2	04		2	32	
3.7	New Cross	6½	5	45	53	6½	6	45	55	6½	6	35	44	6	47	54
											sigs					
6.0	Hither Green	9½	8	25	49	9½	9	23	48	9½	9	23	44	9	24	50
7.8	Grove Park		10	37	47		11	42	42		11	46	40	11	41	43
							pws									
10.1	Chislehurst	16	13	31	51	17	15	30	25	15½	15	08		14	56	46
12.7	ORPINGTON	19	16	22	60	20	19	33	46	19	18	44	50	18	09	54½
15.5	Knockholt		19	28	48		23	30	37		21	49	43	21	24	45
19.5	Dunton Green		23	32	68		27	57	59		25	58	72	25	29	69
21.0	SEVENOAKS T.H.	29	24	58	56	31	29	39	44	29	27	14	66	27	00	50
25.9	Hildenborough		29	44	74		34	25	84		31	34	83	31	59	74
			sigs												sigs	
28.4	TONBRIDGE★	37	32	58	34	39	36	53	33	37½	33	56	35	34	35	28
31.7	High Brooms		38	53	35		42	53	32		40	39	31	41	36	30
			sigs													
33.3	TUNBRIDGE W.C.	47½	42	04		49	46	10		48	43	35		44	52	
Estimated net time (mins)			41				44¾				43¼				44½	

★Speed restriction

49. No. 30923 'Bradfield' bursts out of Somerhill Tunnel with a down Hastings train.

D. W. Winkworth

being set up right through to London Bridge instead of the customary start under yellow signal aspects. The combination of reduced load (an outcome of the signal-box fire at Cannon Street) and late start helped in a fine climb to Knockholt. After Sevenoaks no. 30914 had to be reined-in, but even so a four-minute early arrival at the Wells was noteworthy. Detail B, with no. 30926, is again one of Mr Nash's recordings and confirms that the engines with the original exhaust arrangements could run well enough, in this case to produce the highest speed in the table. Driver Baldock and no. 30909 (detail C), timed by Sir J. Colyer-Fergusson had an unchecked run apart from slight signals and put it to good use especially after Knockholt. In the last detail no. 910 made a particularly brisk climb to Knockholt, and to have pushed its luck too far with fast running would have only made the check it did suffer at Tonbridge more severe.

The schedule in this case was 47½ minutes as for detail A.

In the up direction there is not a lot of data available. Mr D. F. Howard sampled the 8.18 am from Tunbridge Wells on 10 August 1953 having no. 30905 on the customary eleven carriages (349/370 tons), when the 50-minute schedule was bettered by 10 seconds despite signal checks in the London area. A speed of 36 mph was maintained up to Sevenoaks Tunnel and Sevenoaks was passed in 20½ minutes, Knockholt in 27½ minutes, Orpington in 30¾ minutes and Grove Park in 35½ minutes at 69 mph. Net time was 47 minutes.

Performance south of Tunbridge Wells features in table 18. In detail A no. 30926 was heading the Saturday 1.2 pm from Cannon Street with driver Baldock at the regulator. Mr B. I. Nathan timed this enterprising gallop which knocked five minutes off the schedule. In detail

50. On a snowy January Saturday in 1952 no. 30936 'Cranleigh' powers a midday down Hastings refreshment car express past Chislehurst.

Brian Morrison

Table 18. TUNBRIDGE WELLS CENTRAL – CROWHURST

	A 10 Dec. 1955 30926 9 293 310			B 24 Feb. 1950 30905 11 357 375		Detail Date Locomotive no. Vehicles Tare load (tons) Gross load (tons)		C 23 Feb. 1957 30911 8 255 265			D 11 July 1953 30931 (L) 10 325 340	
Mls	Sch.	m. s.	Spd	Sch.	m. s.	Spd	Mls	Sch.	m. s.	Spd	Sch.	m. s.	Spd
0.0	0	0 00		0	0 00		TUNBRIDGE WELLS C.	23.3	34	31 16		24	20 20
										sigs		
2.3		5 17	44		6 08	45	Frant	21.0		26 50	51		17 10	51
4.9		8 34	43		9 10	54	Wadhurst★	18.4	27	23 34	37	16	14 00	38
9.5		13 33	70		13 51	69/80	Stonegate	13.8		17 14	50		8 02	48
13.1	18	16 14	79	19	17 37		ETCHINGHAM	10.2	15	13 26	61	4	3 58	54
15.2		17 52	73		4 37	47	ROBERTSBRIDGE	8.1		11 24	67	0	0 00
18.3		20 52	61		—		Mountfield Halt	4.9		8 05	45		
21.2	28	23 54	47	12	—		Battle	2.1		4 56	53/59		
23.3	32	27 02		16	16 21		CROWHURST★	0.0	0	0 00			

★Speed restriction

93

Table 19. SEVENOAKS TUBS HILL – CANNON STREET

Detail	A	B	C	D
Date	2 June 1949	8 Mar. 1948	9 Mar. 1948	16 Mar. 1948
Train	8.16 am	8.7 am	8.7 am	8.7 am
Locomotive no.	906	902	906	909 (L)
Vehicles	11	11	11	11
Tare load (tons)	350	350	350	350
Gross load (tons)	368	368	368	368
Recorder	R. C. Riley	Author	Author	Author

Mls			Sch.	m. s.	Sch.	m. s.	m. s.	m. s.
0.0	0.0	SEVENOAKS TUBS HILL	0	0 00	0	0 00	0 00	0 00
1.6		Dunton Green		2 17				
5.5		Knockholt		7 38				
6.8		Chelsfield		9 14				
8.3		ORPINGTON	11	10 31				
	1.2	Sevenoaks Bat & B.★				2 40	2 35	2 42
	2.8	Otford				4 39	4 38	5 02
	4.2	Shoreham				6 38	6 30	7 06
	6.4	Eynsford★				8 57	8 53	9 24
								sig. stop
	9.4	SWANLEY JUNCTION				12 37	12 30	15 50
	12.1	St Mary Cray				15 48	15 27	19 28
						sig. stop		
10.9	14.5	Chislehurst	14	12 43		21 28	19 09	22 57
14.9	18.6	Hither Green	19	16 13	28	26 02	23 30	27 42
						sigs		
17.2	20.9	New Cross	22	18 52	31	29 25	26 34	31 00
				sigs			sigs	
20.2	23.9	LONDON BRIDGE	27½	23 33	36½	33 53	32 22	35 16
20.9	24.6	CANNON STREET	31	26 19	40	35 50	34 30	36 39
Estimated net time (mins)				24½		32½	32	33

★Speed restriction

B there is a record of the sort of work the 5.6 pm from Cannon Street did beyond Tunbridge Wells and certainly the sprint to Etchingham was lively. The Saturday 3.30 pm train from Hastings appears in detail C and Mr Nathan had the gratification of logging a good run, albeit with an eight-coach train. Finally no. 30931 was working the 10.10 am from Hastings which Mr M. Hedges noted as leaving Robertsbridge five minutes late; with 58 mph before Stonegate a good climb was made to Wadhurst for the lateness to be substantially cut by the time the train arrived at Tunbridge Wells.

Sevenoaks to Cannon Street might be thought to be an odd length to conclude the post-war performance review of the class,

51. A typical Hastings direct scene. No. 30935 'Sevenoaks' approaches Wadhurst with the 4.50 pm Hastings—Charing Cross train on 25 May 1957.

D. W. Winkworth

especially as table 19 deals solely with the 6.58 am from Hastings leaving Sevenoaks at 8.16 am. Delays in getting passengers on at Hildenborough and Sevenoaks would often lead to a late departure and, unless the train could get in front of the 8.31 am from Bromley North (there was less than three minutes headway at Grove Park), a 10-minute late arrival would be inevitable after trailing behind the Bromley local. Detail A could be described as a typical run; $4\frac{3}{4}$ minutes late leaving Sevenoaks, $1\frac{1}{4}$ minutes clawed back by Chislehurst and then, with the electric train doubtless waiting to come off the branch at Grove Park as no. 906 thundered by, a further gain for the City commuters to be decanted on time at Cannon Street.

Closure of Polhill Tunnel in the spring of 1948 for engineering work meant a diversion for the main line trains via Otford, and to maintain normal arrival times all business trains had departures from Sevenoaks advanced. Working became disorganised at times and consequently late departures were rife; in details B, C and D the trains were $5\frac{1}{4}$, $6\frac{1}{2}$ and $2\frac{1}{4}$ minutes late away respectively yet, over a comparatively unfamiliar switchback road (three summits, two valleys) graded at a constant 1 in $101\frac{1}{2}$, the drivers reduced the deficit to a minute in the first two cases and got in early in the third. This was typical of the work which put the Schools – and the St Leonards representatives in particular – in the forefront of not only Southern Region but also British Railways performance at the time.

95

9
Liveries

Green – be it sage, malachite, olive or Brunswick – was the livery colour most closely associated with the Schools class during the thirty or so years of its existence. Admittedly there were two unfortunate intrusions by black but that is not the hue by which the engines are best remembered.

Sage-green, adopted by the Southern Railway as the standard livery shortly after Grouping had taken place, was the colour in which each member of the class first appeared. Lining-out was in black and white and the lettering was applied in chrome yellow. Although the smokebox, smokebox platform and cab roof were all finished in black, the cylinders, steps and protection guards over the rear wheels of the bogie shared the green and were lined out. Buffer beams, both of engine and tender, were painted

red and carried the locomotive number and 'E' prefix. Nos 900 and 901 were the only engines to have this notation in shaded block style and in due course this was altered to the style which became standard on the railway. The nameplates, numberplates on cab sides and tender back each had a red ground. The power classification letter A was painted on the framing immediately behind the engine buffer beam each side.

When, in mid-1931, the 'E' prefix to the numbers was abolished, 'No.' took its place on the engine buffer beams, new cab side numberplates were fitted, and the tender lost numberplate and buffer beam numbering, merely having the engine number (without 'No.' preceding it) painted on centrally. The second and third batches of the class were turned out new in this fashion and with smoke deflectors painted

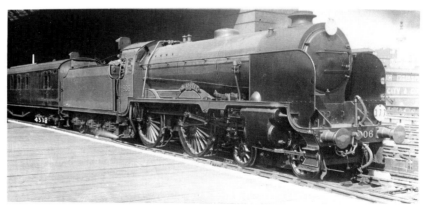

52. Not every engine decked out in the new malachite-green had the distinctive 9-inch high numerals applied to the buffer beam as this picture of no. 906 'Sherborne' at Cannon Street demonstrates.

D. W. Winkworth Collection

96

By courtesy of K. Rogers (J. G. Sturt Collection)

53.   In contradistinction to 'Sherborne' in the previous illustration, no. 908 'Westminster' was adorned with the new lettering and numerals combined with the old green livery. This photograph, depicting no. 908 assisting no. 905 'Tonbridge' on a down Hastings line train at London Bridge, also highlights the large round Isothermos axle boxes on the tender of no. 908 which were a feature of this engine for many years.

54.   The comma in the number, bestowed by Brighton works on 'Charterhouse', was unique for the class.

Lens of Sutton

97

55. Early in BR days 'Leatherhead', seen at Brighton, boasted small numerals on the cab side and Southern style lettering on the tender.

J. Hodgson Collection

black. When nos 900 to 909 acquired smoke deflectors these were finished likewise. The only amendment which took place in this first livery was the lining-out of the cylinders in a panel instead of vertical lining at front and back edges. This was introduced in 1938, and amongst those so treated were nos 900, 901, 902 and 909. The combination of sage-green livery and standard large-diameter chimney was confined to no. 931.

The established sage-green livery of the Schools and the Southern in general was rudely breached at the end of June and the beginning of July 1938 when six Bournemouth-based engines were repainted a light green with new style lettering. Nos 925, 927, 928, 929, 930 and 932 were the six engines concerned. At first the

colour was termed Bournemouth green because it was intended to be used in conjunction with services on that route, but later it became known as malachite. In general those areas previously painted green just changed the shade and were lined out in black and white. An exception to this was no. 928 which had the cylinders painted black. The number plates were replaced by new style numerals and the tender just bore 'SOUTHERN' on each side which, except for no. 932 which had a high-sided tender, was in line with the cab numerals. The front buffer beam figures were larger than used hitherto, or as now applied to the cab sides, and the abbreviation 'No.' was dropped. In August no. 926 also emerged from Eastleigh works so adorned and, with 70 per cent of the Bournemouth engines in the new livery, there was then a sufficient

Rev. A. C. Cawston

56.   No. 30913 'Christ's Hospital' had Gill Sans lettering and numerals applied to the malachite-green livery before the lined black livery was adopted for the class.

number available to power the similar liveried trains.

Application of the new style of lettering and numbering in conjunction with the still standard livery of sage-green was the next development. This occurred in November 1938 when no. 908 was the first Schools to have this treatment. No. 908 retained green cylinders but subsequently nos 914, 923, 924, 933 and 934 were turned out with black cylinders and the old style of numerals on the buffer beam. It is not

without interest that this batch of six engines included two (nos 924 and 933) from Bournemouth shed which might have been expected to reappear in the new livery. However, conceding that there would be a requirement for some of the Bournemouth-based locomotives to work trains in the old livery, this did not upset the premise of the new livery being confined to selected Bournemouth line trains: that is, until the spring of 1939, when nos. 906, 921, 937 and 938 all came out repainted in malachite-green and no. 912 was decked out in olive- (or Dover) green so destroying any semblance of a

57. There were some variations in lining-out in the BR black livery. Here no. 30916 'Whitgift' has lining round the cab window and on the cylinder casing but not on the splashers. Eventually the lining was standardised as along the framing, a rectangle on the tender, a panel beneath the cab window, boiler bands and wheel splashers.

plan for Schools class liveries. No. 912 had green smoke deflectors and black cylinders, nos 906 and 921 had black smoke deflectors and green cylinders, no. 938 black cylinders and no. 937 black cylinders and green smoke deflectors, as well as large numerals on the buffer beam. In all cases the green smoke deflectors were painted in a panel with a horizontal bottom lined edge. A further variation was introduced in some instances in the form of green and yellow lining.

This springtime fever of indecision, vacillation or just plain experimentation subsided in June 1939 when no. 913 reappeared from overhaul in malachite-green, black and yellow lining, black cylinders and green panelled smoke deflectors, all of which added up to the standard malachite-green livery. There was a brief scare in February–June 1940 when seven engines, including no. 927 which had been in malachite-green, were repainted olive-green. Perhaps it was a case of using up surplus stocks of the olive-green paint!

Wartime unlined black livery was first introduced to the class in April 1942 when no. 906 came out of works so garbed, the only concession to colour being green shaded letters and

100

numerals, the same style of numerals on the cab sides being used for the buffer beam. This standard persisted for nearly four years until January 1946 when no. 934 became the first of the class to come out in the post-war malachite-green livery which could be distinguished from that of pre-war by unlined black instead of lined green for the steps and bogie wheel covers.

Nationalisation naturally was to bring changes. At first the malachite-green continued with 'BRITISH RAILWAYS' cramped on to the tender sides instead of 'SOUTHERN', albeit in the same style. Three of the class (nos 914, 934 and 938) got the 'S' prefix applied in front of the numerals, but in about half the numeral height, before the edict to add 30000 to the numbers was issued. 'Charterhouse' appeared as no. 30,903 thanks to Brighton works, which rather liked this style of notation in the first flush of renumbering. Although the engine ran for some time in that condition, the commas did disappear after a while from the numbers on the cab sides but remained in that on the back of the tender! Introduction of cast numberplates on the smokebox door meant that the buffer beam numerals had to disappear, though not before some engines had sported both at the same time. When the British Railways Gill Sans lettering became standard, engines appeared with numerals and lettering of that description.

Eventually it was decreed that the Schools should be finished in BR lined black and so, in September 1948, no. 30923 was the first to show the world what that meant. The red, cream and grey lining appeared to present problems as to where it should be applied; at first the customary method of taking the lining right up and around the cab window and around the perimeter of the tender sides was adopted, only to give way in 1949 to a panel beneath the cab window and, later still, to an oblong panel on the tender side, the top horizontal line being just below the inward break of the tender sheeting. 'BRITISH RAILWAYS' was applied to the tender sides to start with, then these were left blank until the large lion-and-wheel emblem became standard finish giving way to a smaller size after a time. The cylinders were lined vertically front and back and lining-out of the driving wheel splashers was introduced after a few months. Tenders had the engine number painted on the back very unobtrusively and the 'A' power classification was transferred to underneath the number on the cab sides, where later the BR classification 5P also made its appearance, in this instance above the engine number.

This livery did duty for about eight years until belated recognition was given to the class by bestowing upon it the Brunswick green lined with black and orange. First to receive it was no. 30907 in July 1956; the lining on the cab sides was not continuous, the lower part of the panel going straight into the curve of the running plate, following an amendment that had crept in from Ashford. The new type of emblem was, eventually, applied to the tender sides. This final livery did not, however, embrace the whole class as nos 30900, 30914, 30919 and 30932 never acquired it.

10
Preservation

By the time the first Schools engine was withdrawn, the British Transport Commission had already decided upon preserving an example of the class, while the private sector of the preservation movement was in business on the Bluebell Railway and engaged in saving individual locomotives – admittedly of the smaller types rather than express passenger examples. There was, therefore, a commitment for one of the class to avoid the scrap heap and a good chance, if withdrawals did not proceed too rapidly, for another one or two to live on under private auspices.

In the event, withdrawals of the class (apart from the first two in January 1961) took place in the comparatively short space of nineteen months, with no less than seventeen going in the final month in the interests of an accountants' jamboree. This curtailed the expected period of time in which private interests could make arrangements to save one of the class.

Parts of the locomotives did avoid the torch. Of the nameplates, one example from each withdrawn engine was often presented to the school concerned; at least fifteen of the boilers were sold for further use, and tenders nos 723 and 731 were converted to snow-plough carriers (DS 70210 and 70211) in January 1964, followed by six more later on. No. 30933 'King's-Canterbury' fell to the scrappers after a long wait at Ashford during which time efforts were made, by Canterbury City Council as well as the school, to save it for posterity. Other efforts by schools to save their 'own' engines came to naught or never got off the ground.

Doyen of the class 'Eton' had been altered by the addition of the Lemaitre exhaust and large chimney, and was not in particularly good condition in its final months, factors which doubtless caused it to be passed over in favour of an unmodified member of the class – which turned out to be no. 30925 'Cheltenham' – for the honour of official preservation. Upon withdrawal in December 1962 no. 30925 was sent to Fratton for storage to await its turn in the queue for restoration and placing in the national collection.

The first Schools to be privately preserved was no. 30928 'Stowe'. Withdrawn in November 1962, it was purchased by Lord Montagu and transferred from rail to road at Millbrook on 14 February 1964 arriving at Beaulieu the same day, still in British Railways green livery. Lord Robertson of Oakridge performed an inauguration ceremony on 24 March 1964 at the Montagu Motor Museum, of the 'Bournemouth Belle' – which comprised no. 30928 and three Pullman coaches. Of course 'Stowe' never operated that train in BR days, nor yet in Southern years, and later, when repainted in Southern style and given an out-of-time headboard, the illusion seemed even more remote, especially as the AWS gear was still attached!

58. Still unmistakably a Schools despite the removal of buffers, the quaint lining-out of the smoke deflectors and the acquisition of headlight, centre-coupler, cow-catcher, bell and sundry plumbing items for air braking! No. 926 'Repton' heads a three-car consist on the Cape Breton Steam Railway, Nova Scotia, Canada in 1974.

Competing claims for space between a steam railway engine and automobiles were obviously weighted in favour of the road vehicles, and so on 30 November 1972 'Stowe' was moved out, by road, to Marchwood from whence the journey to Eastleigh diesel depot was completed by rail on 12 February 1973. Restoration to original Southern style livery took place and, now jointly owned by Lord Montagu and Mr David Shepherd, the artist, 'Stowe' was towed away from Eastleigh on 17 November 1973 to arrive at Cranmore (East Somerset Railway) the following day. Unfortunately the sojourn exposed to the elements in Hampshire resulted in

the middle cylinder becoming seized up; with little capacity at Cranmore for heavy repairs and less labour resources, no. 928 remained immobile. On 10 July 1980 it arrived at Sheffield Park on the Bluebell Railway on extended loan and started to undergo overhaul, and in less than a year it had been made operational to delight travellers between Horsted Keynes and Sheffield Park.

No. 30926 'Repton', withdrawn at the same time as no. 30925, also went to Fratton shed for storage and, following inquiries from prospective purchasers in North America, was reserved for possible acquisition and eventually – in December 1964 – returned to Eastleigh Works. Purchase and restoration to the original Southern Railway livery followed and in April 1967 'Repton' was towed to Liverpool to be

59. Restored to near post-war Southern Railway
condition just in time for Rainhill 1980 no. 925
'Cheltenham' prepares to take part in the parade.

Mike Esau

shipped to Montreal en route for Steamtown, Bellows Falls, Vermont. Disappointingly, display was in the open and static; by 1974 this was remedied with no. 926 being placed on loan for working the two-month season on the short Cape Breton Steam Railway between Glace Bay and Port Morien in Nova Scotia, Canada. For this purpose a North American type centre-coupler was fitted together with headlight and cow-catcher, and an air pump was installed in front of the smokebox. One can forgive this disfigurement in the effort to make 'Repton' the first of the Schools to come alive again, if only on a limited length of railway for a short period each year.

Guarded reports, however, hint at lack of

maintenance and even unserviceability in Nova Scotia; provided agreement can be reached on responsibility for repairs it does seem possible that 'Repton' could return south and be used to work trains at Steamtown's new location at Kingston, N.Y.

No. 30925 'Cheltenham' left Fratton on 20 September 1964 when it started on a journey to Stratford (London) Works where it arrived the following day. In February 1968 a return to Southern metals was made, residence being taken up at Preston Park (Brighton) on the 20th of that month. Its nomadic existence continued on 9 September 1970 when it left for the Standard Gauge Steam Trust, Tyseley (Birmingham), being on show there a week later. 'Cheltenham' languished at Tyseley, without receiving hoped-for attention, until the

S. C. Nash

60. The distinction of being the first Schools to return to regular revenue-earning service in England belongs to no. 928 'Stowe' for on 13 June 1981 the engine was recommissioned by Lord Montagu of Beaulieu in a ceremony at Horsted Keynes on the Bluebell Railway. It is seen here the day following in full throat!

Department of Education and Science moved it to the Dinting Railway Centre (near Glossop) where it found lodging on 30 January 1973, still in BR green livery. It went on show for a day at Reddish on 9 September 1973 but only received external attention at Dinting until it was called forward to York Railway Museum where it arrived on the last day of October 1977.

Repaired in time to appear in the 'Rocket 150' celebrations at Rainhill in late May 1980, it was finished in the Southern Railway post-war malachite-green livery as no. 925. The AWS gear had been removed, but the BR speedometer remained incongruously in position. Later in the year a return was made to Dinting on loan, only to retrace its way to York where it was placed on display in the Museum in the spring of 1981. It is hoped that eventually it will undergo overhaul to enable it to power special passenger trains on BR metals.

These three engines keep the Schools banner flying but nothing will dim the memory of the sight of 'Blundell's' climbing up through Otterbourne cutting on the 'Bournemouth Limited' all in shining malachite-green, of 'Whitgift' running into Herne Bay on a hot summer Saturday afternoon at the head of the 'Kentish Belle', or of 'Bradfield' blasting its way out of Somerhill Tunnel on a down Hastings express.

Appendix
Construction, Modification and Withdrawal Dates

No.	900	901	902	903	904	905	906	907	908
To traffic	3/30	3/30	4/30	4/30	5/30	5/30	6/30	7/30	7/30
Malachite-green livery	—	10/40	—	9/41	1/40	10/39	4/39	11/40	8/41
Olive-green livery	6/40	—	3/40	—	—	—	—	—	—
Flaman recorder	—	—	—	10/38	12/38	11/38	4/39	9/39	11/38
Lemaitre exhaust	6/40	10/40	—	—	—	—	—	11/40	—
Black livery	1/43	12/43	3/43	11/43	5/42	10/42	4/42	9/44	10/44★
Malachite-green livery	12/46	—	6/46	3/46	5/46	12/46	3/46	3/46	—
Snifting valves removed	3/49	9/48	2/50	1/47	2/49	8/49	11/49	6/48	5/49
S prefix	—	—	—	—	—	—	—	—	—
BR renumbering	5/48	10/48	1/49	3/48	6/48	9/49	12/49	8/48	3/49
BR black livery	10/50	10/48	3/50	5/50	1/51	9/49	12/49	1/52	6/49
BR green livery	—	6/60	4/59	2/59	11/58	8/58	5/58	7/56	8/56
AWS gear	—	6/60	4/59	—	—	—	5/62	—	6/59
Speedometer	1/60	6/60	—	—	—	11/60	11/60	12/59	—
Withdrawn	2/62	12/62	12/62	12/62	7/61	12/61	12/62	9/61	9/61
Cut-up	3/62	8/63	K	2/64	9/61	2/62	4/63	9/61	10/61
Cut-up at	AFD	ELH	K	ELH	AFD	ELH	ELH	AFD	ELH

Names

900	ETON	907	DULWICH	914	EASTBOURNE
901	WINCHESTER	908	WESTMINSTER	915	BRIGHTON
902	WELLINGTON	909	St. PAUL'S	916	WHITGIFT
903	CHARTERHOUSE	910	MERCHANT TAYLORS	917	ARDINGLY
904	LANCING	911	DOVER	918	HURSTPIERPOINT
905	TONBRIDGE	912	DOWNSIDE	919	HARROW
906	SHERBORNE	913	CHRIST'S HOSPITAL		

909	910	911	912	913	914	915	916	917	918	919
8/30	12/32	12/32	12/32	12/32	12/32	5/33	6/33	6/33	7/33	7/33
2/41	8/39	—	8/41	6/39	—	10/40	12/39	—	—	5/39
—	—	3/40	4/39	—	—	—	—	5/40	5/40	—
9/39	—	—	—	—	1/39	—	—	5/39	10/38	10/38
2/41	—	—	—	—	1/39	10/40	—	5/40	5/40	2/41
3/44	11/42	7/42	7/44	1/45	8/43	7/43	9/44★	1/43	5/43	4/43
10/47	—	4/46	4/47	9/48	6/46	—	1/46	2/46	9/46	5/46
9/47	11/48	7/49	2/49	6/48	2/48	8/47	9/48	3/48	8/46	11/49
—	—	—	—	—	3/48	—	—	—	—	—
1/49	12/48	8/49	3/49	9/48	5/50	2/49	11/48	5/48	10/49	8/48
12/50	12/48	8/49	5/50	1/52	5/50	2/49	11/48	7/52	10/49	12/49
8/58	8/56	12/58	5/60	6/59	—	4/57	4/58	8/59	5/57	—
—	6/60	—	5/60	6/59	4/59	8/60	—	8/59	4/59	—
12/60	—	10/60	5/60	—	—	8/60	12/59	—	—	—
1/62	11/61	12/62	11/62	1/62	7/61	12/62	12/62	11/62	10/61	1/61
3/62	1/62	9/63	12/62	2/62	9/61	11/63	9/63	4/63	11/61	3/61
AFD	ELH	ELH	ELH	ELH	AFD	ELH	ELH	ELH	ELH	AFD

Notes: A – Also 6/41

D – Stone Deuta speedometer 8/38

K – Sold 3/64 Geo. Cohen & Co. Kettering and cut-up there shortly after

P – Preserved

★ – Date assessed

References are to month and year. Thus 3/30 indicates March 1930.

No.	920	921	922	923	924	925	926	927	928
To traffic	11/33	11/33	12/33	12/33	12/33	5/34	6/34	6/34	6/34
Malachite-green livery	—	3/39	10/39	9/41	9/40	6/38	8/38	6/38A	7/38
Olive-green livery	3/40	—	—	—	—	—	—	2/40	—
Flaman recorder	10/38	3/39	10/39	12/38	2/39	5/39	11/39	—	9/39
Lemaitre exhaust	3/40	1/41	—	—	9/40	—	—	—	—
Black livery	4/42	4/44	1/45	2/44	6/43	3/43	5/44	9/43	4/42
Malachite-green livery	8/47	1/48	8/46	7/46	10/47	1/48	11/46	8/47	6/48
Snifting valves removed	7/47	12/47	11/48	7/48	9/47	12/47	3/49	10/49	5/48
S prefix	—	—	—	—	—	—	—	—	—
BR renumbering	10/48	3/50	1/49	9/48	1/49	5/50	4/48	11/49	6/48
BR black livery	11/49	3/50	1/49	9/48	10/50	5/50	4/49	11/49	6/49
BR green livery	9/57	1/59	1/57	12/57	9/59	1/60	10/60	3/58	7/59
AWS gear	—	10/61	—	—	—	1/60	10/60	5/60	7/59
Speedometer	—	—	—	—	—	1/60	10/60	11/59	—
Withdrawn	11/61	12/62	11/61	12/62	1/62	12/62	12/62	1/62	11/62
Cut-up	1/62	K	12/61	8/63	1/62	P	P	4/62	P
Cut-up at	AFD	K	AFD	ELH	AFD	—	—	ELH	—

Names

920	RUGBY	926	REPTON	933	KING'S-CANTERBURY
921	SHREWSBURY	927	CLIFTON	934	St. LAWRENCE
922	MARLBOROUGH	928	STOWE	935	SEVENOAKS
923	BRADFIELD	929	MALVERN	936	CRANLEIGH
	(UPPINGHAM until 8/34)	930	RADLEY	937	EPSOM
924	HAILEYBURY	931	KING'S-WIMBLEDON	938	St OLAVE'S
925	CHELTENHAM	932	BLUNDELL'S	939	LEATHERHEAD

929	930	931	932	933	934	935	936	937	938	939
8/34	12/34	1/35	2/35	3/35	3/35	6/35	6/35	7/35	7/35	8/35
6/38	6/38	7/40	7/38	5/40	3/41	5/39	7/39	5/39	2/39	8/40
—	—	—	—	—	—	—	—	—	—	—
6/39	—	11/38	—	12/38	—	—	—	—	—	D
3/41	4/40	7/39	—	5/40	5/40	—	—	5/39	6/40	8/40
1/44	11/42	12/42	8/45	10/43	5/45	9/43	5/44	12/45	1/44★	3/43
—	7/48	—	7/48	6/48	1/46	—	9/46	9/48	3/46	4/48
7/47	6/48	2/48	6/48	4/48	1/48	11/48	7/48	12/47	1/49	5/47
—	—	—	—	—	3/48	—	—	—	3/48	—
1/49	7/48	10/48	7/48	6/48	9/48	12/48	7/48	9/48	3/49	4/48
1/49	3/50	10/48	2/51	6/51	1/50	12/48	3/49	12/50	3/49	10/50
12/56	10/56	10/58	—	6/58	2/60	12/56	4/61	1/57	10/56	3/57
8/61	4/60	—	—	—	5/62	6/59	11/59	9/60	—	10/59
1/60	4/60	1/60	—	—	2/60	5/60	11/59	9/60	3/60	—
12/62	12/62	9/61	1/61	11/61	12/62	12/62	12/62	12/62	7/61	6/61
3/63	4/64	10/61	8/61	12/61	8/63	K	10/63	6/63	9/61	9/61
ELH	ELH	AFD	AFD	AFD	ELH	K	ELH	ELH	AFD	AFD

Index